T0113690

Welcome To My World Of Animal Communication And Healing

Maureen Rolls

authorHOUSE®

AuthorHouse™ UK
1663 Liberty Drive
Bloomington, IN 47403 USA
www.authorhouse.co.uk
Phone: UK TFN: 0800 0148641 (Toll Free inside the UK)
UK Local: (02) 0369 56322 (+44 20 3695 6322 from outside the UK)

Published by AuthorHouse 09/29/2022

ISBN: 978-1-7283-7517-5 (sc)
ISBN: 978-1-7283-7519-9 (e)

Print information available on the last page.

This book is printed on acid-free paper.

Contents

INTRODUCTION

I was born into a family of nine children, three boys and four girls (including me). One of my brothers contracted meningitis and died, and another brother was stillborn. Being the youngest in a very large family of nine, all meat eaters, was a daily struggle for me. I recall from a very young age refusing to eat any meat. My mum, throughout my childhood, persisted in trying to change that; however, I always refused. After an exhaustible amount of trying to persuade me to eat the meat on my plate, Mum eventually relented and took me to our doctor. When we arrived at the surgery, the doctor remarked, 'Is she thinner than the other children?' My mother said I wasn't. He further enquired; 'Does she get ill more than the other children?' My mum said I didn't. He then said, 'Please do not worry about her. Allow her to eat what she wants within reason.' From then on, my parents never tried to force me to eat meat again. This was the first step of my journey, strongly indicating to me I had come to this planet to teach people how to communicate with animals and help every species through my natural gift.

Sadly, for many centuries, humans have abused and mistreated animals dreadfully. Some treat them as if they were no more than machines, not considering they may have feelings or even have souls. In fact, I have been told numerous times that animals do not have souls. How misinformed and small minded certain people can be to believe humans are the only living creatures to have souls. I feel saddened to think this opinion is accepted in many society by people who do not have the kindness of love and compassion within their hearts to see their error.

For as long as I can remember, I have had a heart and soul connection with animals, a deep friendship that goes beyond just this life. They have always been something that I feel safe with; I can relate to them. I find this feeling reciprocated as animals relate to me with ease too. When I was very young, dogs, cats, and all sorts of other animals came to me for help. I would openly communicate with them, helping and sometimes healing those who asked me to. In my childish naivety, I thought that everyone could communicate with animals; however, when I started talking about it to other children, I was laughed at and ridiculed. It didn't take me long to swiftly realise that not every child could communicate as easily as I could. My gift of communication was just that, a present for my future to come.

So, for many years, from my childhood right up until I was in my late forties and early fifties, I did not let people know that I communicated with animals. I communicated with them throughout my entire life; I just didn't publicise it or talk to people about it. I just did what I needed to do for the animals without letting any humans know about it. This led me onto a path in my adult life of outwardly helping animals that were in trouble and needed my assistance.

Living on Dartmoor, which is in southern Devon in the Southwest of Britain, I was accustomed to animals like badgers, foxes, and feral ponies roaming on the moor. It was not unusual for me to have a pony turn up outside my home. On one particular occasion, a mare arrived needing desperate help for her foals. Once the mare let me know she needed me, she collapsed and died outside my house. She left a new-born foal, which was only a few days old, and her yearling, which was still with her at foot. The mare had instinctively led them to my home, somehow knowing they would be cared for and safe.

This is my life, this is my world, and this is what I am here to do, live my soul journey. I feel I have been here on this planet many times before, and over my varied past lives, I have evolved to the point where I am on a much higher frequency and a much higher energy level than many other people and animals. In this incarnation, I have been very blessed; it has been a wonderful, wonderful life that I have lived.

There is no false facade with animals. Their nature is their nature and what they live; they are very honest and true to their feelings. When an animal becomes unpleasant maybe nasty, biting, kicking or otherwise aggressive, it is usually the result of what humans have imposed on them. Therefore, I am here to help these animals to cope, understand, and get through it, always positively reinforcing that not all humans are the same.

On occasions, I have not been able to sleep after seeing animals that have been mistreated by humans. This always leaves me really distressed. These feelings have been with me since childhood. When I am in an animal's energy, I feel what the animal feels. I talk to them; I give them visions and receive visions from them. I also give them healing. I do not need to be with an animal to connect, a photograph with their name (if the animal is a pet) is enough for me to tune into the animal's energy communicate fully so I can help it. This amazing gift opens me up to help support animals throughout the world; in fact, I have helped animals in Australia, New Zealand, Italy, Hong Kong, America, Greece, and many other countries. The beauty of my communication is I that I do not need to be with the animals in order to help them. This is not about seeing the physical; it is about believing about energy.

I use the network, the web if you like, and I don't mean the Internet, the universal web of energy that links us all together. It links those who are on this side of the world as well as those who are on the other. Energy is what I work with, and energy is what the animals understand, much more than humans do. As a child, I had not realised that I could feel animals' energies, and I was also surprised that I could connect deeply to how they felt.

One day, as an older child, I was walking through Camels Head, (an area in Plymouth, England,) a beautiful Persian cat ran across the road and got hit by a car. I instantly felt the trauma of that incident as well as the pain that poor cat felt, I felt it too 100%. I started crying uncontrollably and I continued to cry for several days. I had been unaware that I had linked into this dear cat who sadly died after the accident because of the force of the car hitting him. The pain stayed with me.

However, what I didn't realise till much later was that, when working with the energy of an animal or human, it is important to tune into it and make a connection. Then it is just as important to close that connection by bringing yourself back out of it. This must be in addition to making sure you are protected and fully grounded. Nobody had given me this information, simply because there was no one to give it to me. As I continued my experiences working closely with animal energies, I had to learn, and I have carried that lesson on through all my life.

Being naive to energy as a child and watching as the Persian cat was killed, I realised I had connected deeply with it. I felt the acute pain as the car hit the cat, and I felt overwhelming sadness. These emotions carried with me for several days after the incident. Nobody in my family could understand my emotions, especially my mum. I could not explain to them what was going on with me. I didn't understand myself.

Because of my erratic emotions, it was decided that Mum would take me to the doctor. After several visits, I was still breaking out in tears sporadically, and I was not able to control my emotions. The doctor recommended electric shock treatment. At that time, electric shock treatment was seen as a revolutionary treatment for many ailments.

Medical practitioners could not determine the cause of my condition. There was no understanding within society that people could communicate with animals and work with them on an energetic level. Any suggestion of this would have been dismissed immediately, with damning results. People of that era didn't have the open minds necessary to accept the concept of energy.

Sitting down after hearing what the doctor had said, I thought to myself, *Why, why, why am I feeling this?* I then realised that my emotional state was linked back to the day that I saw this dear cat being killed in front of me. I told myself to snap out of this, I didn't want electric shock treatment, but I didn't want to be like this all the time. I didn't want the doctors thinking that I had a mental illness because I didn't! I was very much an empath, and I had picked up on the pain and suffering of the dear animal.

I told myself I needed to shake this off. I needed to pull myself through this and stop holding the energy in and around me. I started in my own way by dismissing the energy away from me, even though I didn't understand what I was doing. As I said, nobody showed me how to do any of this; I was not taught by a spiritual teacher. This all happened during a time when I was becoming aware of being guided. I didn't know who was guiding me; I only knew it was someone in the higher realms (spirit) who was assisting me. I had no understanding of what this entity was or how he or she could help me. I had just accepted that, if I needed help, I would ask, and I would receive the appropriate help I needed. This happened all on an energetic level; it was not about the physical.

When I work with guidance from the higher realms, I am able to communicate with animals. I can give their human guardians information that I previously did not know. I am gifted with visions and feelings. It is as if the animals are speaking to me. When I relay to the animals' guardians what the animals have 'said' to me and shown me, they are amazed. This is purely because there is no way that I would have known the facts I am able to tell them.

As my life continued, I openly connected with energies; however, most of my family members, my father, my brothers and sisters, were very skeptical and very frightened of what I could do. My mother, on the other hand, was a dear old soul who could read tea leaves and conduct seances. She was the person in the street whom everyone would come to if they were ill, giving birth, or if someone had died. Mum would lay people out before the funeral parlour came to pick them up. She would help women give birth before the midwife turned up. The midwife used to tell everyone, 'Call on Mrs. Bickell, and she will help you until I arrive.' Although my mum was a very gentle, dear old soul, she was no fool! You couldn't fool my mum, bless her, and I believe I have taken on a lot of her traits and a lot of her strength. She wasn't aware of her power and strength, but I could see and feel it in all she did

My childhood progressed like that of any other young girl. I started working after I left school at the age of fourteen, all the while dealing with the problems of being a teenager. All through my formative years, I was still able to communicate with animals. They would come up to me in the street, and their guardians would say something like, 'She doesn't do that! She won't go to anyone.' And, yet the animal would come to me. I believe this was because animals could not only feel my energy, but they could also see my aura - my energetic body. Our aura constantly changes, indicating with various colours how we are feeling, how healthy we are, what we're doing, and what kind of work we do. Through animal communication, my energy often glows, and that energetic signal shows animals they can approach me safely when they needed help.

The aura, or energetic body, surrounds the physical body. It can't be seen by the majority of people; however, some people have a psychic gift that enables them to view the aura of every living thing. Most people may only experience the energy of their auras to protect them and to heighten their awareness and their ability to pick up on things. When someone standing next to you in a queue causes you to experience an uncomfortable feeling, that is your aura telling you to be aware and do not trust. Your aura is picking up negativity and letting you know. Likewise, when you fall in love with someone, you feel wonderful when you are with that person, and you experience a feeling of deep connection. That is your aura blending with the aura of your loved one. Most describe it as a wonderful, warm, comfortable feeling. This blending can make you feel euphoric and is often deemed the relationship as destined and meant to be.

Energy connection has enabled me to help animals, whether they are domesticated, feral (wild after once being domesticated), or wild from birth. This includes mammals in the sea and the many indigenous species throughout the globe. For me, there is no end to my ability when communicating with these creatures. I even include birds. It has been such a blessing being able to be here for all these creatures. I have had the privilege of helping them, and, in turn, I have received help many times. I am grateful every day that I have been able to do this, and I thank our dear Lord that I have been gifted with this ability from birth.

My ability to communicate with animals is definitely a gift. We are all born with our brains wide open. When we are babies, there isn't one part of our brain that is not ready to be used, including the psychic area. Being open with no preconceived ideas, we can communicate telepathically and even see things like spirits. This ability is what we are born with.

Very often we will see babies in their cots giggling and kicking their legs. This is because they can see spirit families that come to visit them and play with them. You may not be able to see them; however, babies can.

A child who has an imaginary friend is operating under the same premise. Their 'friends' are not imaginary at all; they are spirits in child or adult form. When you hear a child talking late in the night, usually at around three o'clock, you can guarantee he or she is talking to either family in spirit, archangels, or a guardian angel. In childhood, our brains are still wide open enough to recognise and be able to do this.

Sadly, as soon as we go to school, children who are ridiculed (as I was,) shut off certain parts of their brains. This happens normally when they are told 'Don't be stupid' or 'Don't be silly, that doesn't exist.' People disbelieve the things they can't see, but that doesn't mean those things don't exist. Very sadly, children come to believe that they have been making up their experiences. They don't want to come across to others as mad, weird, or unusual. This results in children shutting down those parts of their brains, and subsequently, they no longer see spirits.

How sad that society sends us to school to learn for our future and then, through fear and prejudice, shuts off the very part of our brains that we are meant to use. As a species, we have denied ourselves so much advancement, especially when we still have the primordial skills and abilities available for us to use to aid our spiritual evolution.

When did this practice of abstinence of the true self start? I suspect back in the Victorian and Edwardian times. Today the world is a much more open place. Children express their thoughts and feelings outwardly. Adults are comfortable to reopen that part of their brains and connect with their true selves. They become psychics, mediums, empaths, and healers. These endeavours are not frowned on anymore. Not everyone believes as I do, however, and that is personal preference. Whatever people believe or don't believe, the divine spirit is working for us and through us without judgement. I will be uncovering further examples on this subject throughout this book.

This introduction has taken me through my life's journey, and now I'd like to explain how I have used my animal communication skills. I have helped badgers that were being maligned and being dug out of their sets for all sorts of dreadful sport. I have helped foxes that were being hunted and killed and dug out of badger sets also in the name of sport. I have also helped feral ponies on the moor. When I moved out to Dartmoor, I was unaware of the issues and the problems that were so bad for these poor ponies. It was not unusual at that time to find mares very emaciated and very weak trying to feed their foals. These normally would be last year's foals still suckling. It was also not unusual for me to find that one of these mares was critically injured after being hit by a car. Unfortunately, in most of these instances, the farmer would come and shoot the mare. He would also shoot her foal if it was not able to fend for itself. The lucky ones might be taken on by a charity or stable. Why does this happen? Simply because people don't want to spend money on vets' bills or spend time and energy bringing up and looking after the foals. The reality to these farmers is its not worth it for them.

I was appalled at this attitude after moving onto Dartmoor and opening my riding school. The situation highlighted for me certain issues on Dartmoor connected to some farmers and their animal care. There were, of course, very conscientious and caring farmers who did take care of their animals. However, there were far too many farmers who would just shoot them without a second thought.

As time passed, if a pony was injured or killed, the public would inform the police. The police, in turn would tell the farmers and then kindly call on me as well. I was so grateful to them for that, as I had a riding school and could help the ponies. Many times, the ponies got into trouble. Ponies can get stuck in gullies. Foals can get stuck in bogs and are often left alone when the herd moves on. The police alerted me to these issues and many more.

One year, there was an outbreak of tetanus (lockjaw), and ponies were being shot instead of being treated. Nobody was even trying to get help from a vet. Seeing the injustice caused by the lack of care for these animals, I became immeasurably frustrated. It was in one of these moments that I decided to start my own charity. I called it South West Equine Protection. I ran this charity for forty years. We assisted moorland ponies that needed help and brought in ponies farmers no longer wanted and were planning to shoot. It was my quest to take these unfortunate animals on and give them love and care.

My charity would happily welcome a foal whose mother had been killed by a car. The farmers would give me the foal to bring up, look after, and care for. In addition to receiving animals, I went out on the moor with my husband to find reported ponies that were in trouble. I would get a vet to come and attend to them. Together we would then decide what was best for the animal, depending on quality of life. If the farmer was agreeable, we would then bring the pony in. The ponies were all owned by farmers who had grazing rights on Dartmoor, and eventually, through the charity's dedication and passion for the ponies' welfare, we got involved with ponies on Bodmin Moor, in Cornwall, as well.

For me, it was a labour of unconditional love being there for the animals on Dartmoor and Bodmin Moor. I ran that charity at the start with my husband. For several years, we paid all expenses, including food and vet bills. We did not have any outside financial help.

When we eventually registered as a charity, we were able to get some volunteers to help us, and our charity grew exponentially. In 2019, when I turned seventy-four, I decided it was time to retire. I approached the Mare and Foal Sanctuary charity, also located in Devon, to see if they would incorporate South West Equine Protection. Thankfully they agreed, and the two merged that year. I remain a trustee of the charity and am still very much involved in rescuing moorland and domesticated ponies.

I originally formed South West Equine Protection because no other charity was helping feral ponies on the moors. I soon found out, through rescue operations, that these moorland ponies were like streetwise kids. They knew every trick in the book. Their instincts were so quick that they developed a sixth sense about what humans might do to them. This instinct was vital because, annually, the ponies would be rounded up. For purposes of identification and proof of ownership, the farmers would hot brand foals or cut bits of flesh out of their ears. The pain the animals went through when receiving the farmers' marks caused the ponies to distrust some humans. That being the case, moorland ponies are very difficult to handle and to break in.

I use a method of working with the ponies called halter breaking, but I don't mean 'cowboy style' breaking, which is what a lot of the farmers practice. I'm talking about 'joining up.' I'm talking about using the energy of the animals to join up with them and allow mutual trust to grow. This is very important and enables people to handle the ponies, halter break them, walk them, pick up their feet for foot care, and groom them. All of this is done through *communication* - a concept that is paramount when working with animals.

Keeping open communication with animals is a must. They not only read the body language of the people around them; they communicate telepathically with one another. And this is exactly what I do, I communicate telepathically to them. They can 'hear' me, they can 'talk' back to me, and I receive some fantastic honest information. So, there is no surprise when I say animals have been the biggest, happiest, and most rewarding part of my life. I don't mind saying that sometimes I have preferred animals to humans. (I still do at times!)

In my later years I had the divine experience of an archangel appearing before me; it was Gabriel. From this pivotal point, I realised that, through my life, it was the archangels who were working with me;

it was their energy that was coming through me and healing the animals. The archangels were also guiding the animals to me when they were in trouble and helping me to find them. Archangels are divine energies of the seventh realm; it's a wonderful feeling being connected with their energy. The archangels are not human; they are pure energy-the energy of Christ. They show themselves in human form with wings so they will not frighten us. I have been immensely proud to work with angelic energy; it enables me to do healing. So, when Archangel Gabriel appeared before me and told me to delegate all my charity work, I listened. The archangels wanted me to show others how to communicate with animals. So, for the last fifteen years, I have been holding animal communication workshops here in Devon, and sometimes further afield depending on where I'm being requested to go.

My workshops take place in just one day. I begin with meditation, which allows participants' brains to reopen to accept the learning they will be given. By the end of the morning, participants are able to communicate with animals via photograph, and in the afternoon, I present two special guest animals with whom participants will communicate and do healing on a one- to-one basis. At the end of the workshop, participants will have achieved varying degrees of learning; everyone is different. Some people who attend are starting at the bottom of the ladder. These are people who are not so quick to pick up on everything but are still able to do it. Others who are already doing psychic work or who just have natural ability (because they have not closed that part of their brains) finish the workshop easily communicating with animals and getting great connections. It is amazing to see people open and connect with the animals as well as the guardians of those animals.

So, one day! That's all it takes for meditation and connecting to an animal spirit guide. This is just my way of saying we can all communicate with animals. It is entirely up to each individual. It is about accepting, believing, and trusting, and if you can do that, there is no earthly or unearthly reason that can keep you from communicating with animals. I am not the only one with this skill. We are all born with our brains wide open, a prerequisite to communicating with animals.

Disclaimer: The events and characteristics of the individual guardians and animals in my book have been written as they naturally occurred. To protect the privacy of some guardians and animals (who are now sadly deceased so I could not obtain their permission,) I have changed the names to ensure anonymity.

Chapter 1

ANGELS AND ARCHANGELS

Angels are the pure energy of God. They are winged messengers from heaven to help earth. The word *angelos* in Greek means messenger. There are various dominions of angels whose own tasks have been laid out to ensure that we, as humans, can call on their help for all aspects of our lives including health and helping our planet. They are links between heaven and earth.

Angels were created with free will, and most of the angels chose to give up this free will to serve God. Those who chose to keep their free will are the fallen angels.

Humans are all born with free will, and nothing can take that away. To request help from any angels, just pray or call upon them for help and assistance. This enables them to appear or to assist you with what you have requested. You must give them permission to help. The only time any angel will interfere with your free will is if you are about to die but it is not your destined time to go. For instance, a car, after an accident, might be a writeoff, but the driver has sustained only cuts and bruises. In this case, the angels have taken the person out of the situation to ensure he or she lives.

Angels sometimes appear to us in human form with wings to ensure that we are not frightened. At other times, they are present as bright light.

Archangels are the powerful overseers of all the angels, and they are of the seventh dimension; only the highest orders of angels dwell there, including thrones, seraphim, and cherubim.

There are many archangels. Each has allocated tasks, and each works with a ray of light that is mostly one colour. I have worked daily with the following archangels all my life.

Archangel Gabrielle (orange ray of light)—creativity and disabling fear

Archangel Chamuel (pink ray of light)—love and compassion

Archangel Raphael (emerald-green ray of light)—harmony and healing

Archangel Zadkiel (purple ray of light)—spiritual growth and self-transformation

Archangel Michael (sapphire-blue ray of light)—communication and protection

There are many more, so take some time to investigate and learn about their purposes and how they can all help you.

We each have a guardian angel allocated to us from birth to death to help and guide us. You can also call on your guardian angel for help and assistance.

Chapter 2

Do Animals Have Souls, Feelings, and Past Lives?

For years, people have believed that animals do not have souls or past lives or any feelings.

Of course they have souls and feelings just as humans do. It's just that animals do not mask their feelings like humans do. Animals are more direct. If they are hurt or upset, they respond accordingly to let us know, usually with behaviour changes. This is why vets cannot resolve behavioural problems in animals, drugs do not help, and neither do training classes.

Most animals just want to be heard and understood. They want their humans to understand what is going on in their bodies.

As an animal communicator, I am usually, as the guardians say, their last resort-so no pressure, especially when the guardians are considering euthanising the animal in question. We must remember that, throughout all of this, animals have free will, so they do not need to listen to me or take my advice. But most animals are just grateful that I am there to help them. They do listen, and they ask me how I can help them. A few have refused my help, and that is fine, they have free will. However, it has only been three out of thousands of animals that have elected to do this.

Most of the behavioural problems are caused by abuse by humans or previous guardians in this life or an earlier one; this is not unusual in horses and dogs who are physically held in captivity and unable to leave. Cats, however, usually are able to leave at the slightest sign that energy is changing for the worse.

Some animals act out to alert their guardians to the fact that they are not listening to them and that there is a health issue with their human that needs attention.

Just as it is with humans, most animals have had past lives, and they come back to experience certain events in order to evolve on their spiritual journey. Horses that have experienced horrors of war have come back to experience love and nurture provided by kind humans. Dogs that have been used for killing and fighting have come back to experience love and care. But they bring lots of issues forward from their past lives, usually as behavioural problems. These problems can start when there is a trigger in their current lives that sets off a sequence of events from a past life in their minds. Some have come back to experience their past-life events with their soul humans.

Lots of animals that I communicate with are currently with their soul humans, and they have been together at least once before and sometimes many times throughout thousands of years. It is also not unusual for the owners to say, 'This is my soul partner. We have such a strong bond, and this animal is part of me.' How true this is. I have seen a dog take the illness of its owner on and await death. This dog told me that was why he was here, it was his journey to do this. He was awaiting death to take the suffering from his guardian, and he knew that they would be together again in another life. I spoke to the guardian to relay this to her. She had been suffering with cancer, but it was in remission. She understood this and asked me to tell the dog not to die for her. She would rather die first, but he would not listen, and he passed away a few weeks later.

Animals, in many instances, are more evolved than we are as humans, and of course, they still obey their natural instincts, which we have lost over the millennia.

Yes, animals do have souls and feelings, and they have had past lives.

Chapter 3

ANIMAL CHAKRAS (ENERGY CENTRES)

All living animals have chakras. These are energy centres in various parts of animal bodies and human bodies.

Chakras exist within the energy field of our bodies, and they work with the physical body. They are pure energy and are funnel shaped. They vibrate all the time.

A blocked chakra can cause a physical issue in the body and can even cause some illnesses, discomfort, and pain.

Chakras are not visible, but some psychic people are gifted and are able to see them or sense that they are blocked or open. Chakras open or close depending on many things. If you are grieving, have just had an operation, have been abused, have just had an argument, are feeling ill, or are in any other state of imbalance, your chakras may close. If you are feeling threatened, you will close certain chakras to protect yourself. It is the same for all the animal species.

In our three-dimensional world, there are seven main chakras:

Base/root chakra - One chakra in the tail area of the body.

Sacral chakra - One at the front of the body and one at the back of the body just below the naval.

Solar plexus - One at the front of the body and one at the back of the body near the end of the rib cage.

Heart chakra - One at the front of the body and one at the back of the body in the heart area.

Throat chakra - One at the front of the throat and one at the back of the throat.

Third eye - One at the front of the head in the middle of the forehead between the eyes, and one at the back of head.

Crown chakra - One enormous chakra on the top of the head that is the connection to the higher realm our Lord God and the angels.

All animals, like humans, are in the throws of transition from the third dimension to the fifth dimension. This means we are just opening up our fifth-dimension chakras to connect to an even higher level of energy and information from the higher realm. This is happening now connecting the other five chakras to a higher frequency and vibration for the enlightenment of the fifth dimension.

These chakras, along with the seven chakras listed above, exist in both animals and humans.

Earth star chakra - Below the root chakra down in the earth below the feet/hooves/paws in the ground.

Naval chakra - Between the sacral chakra and the solar plexus chakra, in the front and back of the body in the naval area.

Casual chakra - Single chakra way above the crown chakra.

Soul star chakra - Single chakra above the casual chakra high up in the Universe

Stellar gateway chakra - Single chakra that is linked and connected to the higher realms and is above the soul star chakra.

These are the twelve chakras of the fifth dimension:

Earth star chakra - Archangel Sandalphon

Base/root chakra - Archangel Uriel

Sacral chakra - Archangel Gabriel

Naval chakra - Archangel Gabriel

Solar plexus - Archangel Jophiel

Heart chakra - Archangel Raphael and Archangel

Chamuel

Throat chakra - Archangel Michael

Third eye chakra - Archangel Raziel

Crown chakra - Archangel Zadkiel

Casual chakra - Archangel Christiel

Soul star chakra - Archangel Mariel

Stellar gateway chakra - Archangel Metatron

When an animal's chakras are working correctly and are not blocked, the animal will be happy and content. If an animal's chakras are blocked, the animal will display behavioural problems and may experience various ailments as well.

An animal that is very aggressive usually has chakras that are blocked and not functioning as they should. But not only the chakras need rebalancing; the issue or problem the animal is holding on to must be resolved.

There are lots more chakras all over the body that can help to alleviate illness and behavioural problems.

Chapter 4

Animals Auras

Animals certainly have auras. Animals can also see each other's auras as well; they use this as part of their communication with each other. It is common to see animals putting their hackles up and growling at other animals and sometimes humans. The reason for this is that they have read the aura of another animal or a human, and they can see it is not the kind, gentle aura that it should be. In other words, they see the individual as a threat. When animals see auras that are weak, they know that the animal is frightened or timid.

Animal auras, like human auras, are indicators of the animal's or human's health and mental state. The auras of animals or humans that have been abused contain weak, submissive colours. Unfortunately, this can make them a target for aggression. Equally, a very strong aura containing dominant colours will be considered a threat.

Animals have souls that will cross over to the other side when they leave this plane. Just like humans, they come back to experience certain events that enable their souls to evolve.

Chapter 5

ANIMALS RAINBOW BRIDGE

When animals' souls leave their bodies, they are helped by an angel who is there to guide them into the light and over the rainbow bridge.

There is a destined time for their lives to end, and the angels are aware of this, so they wait for that destined time to assist these dear souls to cross over into the light. This angel is dedicated to helping all animals and ensuring that they are not frightened, but are feeling nothing but love and peace and tranquillity.

No matter how traumatic or how much pain these dear souls felt on earth, when their souls leave their bodies, all pain, fear, and trauma is taken from them. This ensures that the transition from earth to heaven is wonderful and pain free.

When they reach the other side, there will be deceased family members from their own natural family there to greet and reconnect with them. There will also be some of the guardians' deceased family members who will be there to greet them and help them to adjust to being in spirit and not of the third-world physical form.

When animals and humans die very tragically, their souls are taken to reception for healing. When this process has been completed and the souls have healed, they are taken to re-join deceased family members.

All deformities and pain and earthly ailments disappear; these things do not exist in the higher realm.

Whilst they are in spirit, animals can and do come back to visit you and try to help you from the other side. You may sense their energy around you or feel movement on the bed or other furniture. You may also have a very vivid dream that feels so real, as if the animal was actually with you. Yes, that animal friend was with you. He or she used the dream state to connect to you. You might hear a bark or a meow in the garden or another room. Yes, that is also your animal visiting you. So, take note and listen because this usually happens when your mind is quiet; This is when your animal spirit friends can tune into your mind to give you these signs. Talk to them. They can hear you. You may or may not hear them talk back. If you are still grieving, your mind is not at the right wavelength for you to hear or see this, so try to find peace within yourself and allow your animals to connect with you.

Remember, you cannot change what is destined to be. Everything happens for a reason. You are not to blame for their passing. The human within us just wants to ensure that all is as we want it to be, but destiny has taken the reins, and you are just the observer at this point, so forgive yourself and stop blaming yourself. No one else blames you. Your animal certainly does not. Animals fully understand how this all works out.

Just keep giving yourself lots of love and ask the archangels to help you with this.

How Pets Demonstrate Their Love

All species of animals have their own ways of communicating with humans.

Horses

Horses rush up the field whinnying with their heads held high and tails held high.

They nuzzle you in the back and also wicker.

They put their heads over your shoulder to love you.

Dogs

Dogs jump up with tails wagging to greet you and

They rush around finding their favourite toy to give you.

They jump up on the settee and put their heads on your lap or even roll over to expose their tummies for a tickle (they do this only to those they trust and love.)

Some dogs will lift their lips and smile as a greeting of love. (This is not the aggressive type of lifting the lip and growling.)

Cats

To greet you, cats rush in from outdoors and rub their bodies against your legs. They lie on the floor and roll from side to side.

Cats also are playful and hold you with their claws but not hurt you. They also latch on with their teeth without biting.

They snuggle up on your lap and purr. Sometimes they rub their face against yours as a sign of affection.

All our pets (horses, dogs, and cats) are sensitive to spirits and the energies of the home including gardens and other areas. Some animals are more sensitive than others, and they can see and sense spirits. When they sense unfriendly energies or spirits, very often they try to make you aware through their behaviour.

The signs to look out for:

Family member or friendly spirits:

- The animal sits and stares at the wall or ceiling when there is nothing there that you can see.
- The animal's tail wags, and the animal makes a slight greeting noise whilst looking at a specific area of the room.

- The animal sniffs the air when there is no smell and cocks his or her head from side to side trying to adjust to spirits energy.
- The dog barks and rushes around the room trying to find a favourite toy to give to the spirit; this mostly applies to the spirit of a very close member of the family.

Not so good energy and spirit:

The dog stares and barks aggressively constantly for no reason.

The animal refuses to go into a room or area of the house or garden.

The animal destroys furniture and items of clothing or urinates on everything or even worse defecates everywhere. (If this happens, seek help from a professional to cleanse and remove this entity or spirit, and send it to the light.)

Chapter 7

Animal Communications

I have been an animal communicator all my life, and it never fails to amaze me, even at my age, to realise the amount of knowledge the animals have about their humans and about what is happening in the world. Their psychic ability to know what is about to happen to their guardians is extraordinary. I continue to learn about the animals' knowledge and wisdom and how to communicate with them. I am so thrilled to have been born with this wonderful gift.

I moved out onto Dartmoor and, after realising how many issues there were with the moorland ponies, I opened a riding school. I started a charity called South West Equine Protection (SWEP) which has now been established for the last forty years. When I retired in 2019, I approached the Mare and Foal Sanctuary charity to see if they would be willing to amalgamate SWEP with their own charity. I am pleased to say that this was possible, and I became a trustee for the Mare and Foal Sanctuary to continue to have an input in both charities.

Horse Communication Stories

Snippet, My Animal Spirit Guide

The yard at Merrivale on Dartmoor, called Hillside Riding School, was open to the Moorland Ponies, who were able to wander in and out as they pleased. One morning, a beautiful little Shetland pony arrived at my door with a foal at foot. She was dragging her back leg and extremely emaciated.

I led her to my stables and made her comfortable. As I was very new to the moor at that time, I wasn't sure who she belonged to; my knowledge of who owned the stock on the moor was very limited. I contacted my vet who treated her and told me that all she needed was warmth, food, and tender loving care (TLC,) which is what she got in my stables. She stayed in my stables for the winter with her foal. I fed her up and got her fit and well. Then, in the spring, I released her onto the moor. I called her Snippet because the farmer who owned her had cut her tail so short it was right up to the dock. Unfortunately, he also cut her mane very short, which meant she had no means of keeping the flies off, a cruel act really. Every year, after giving birth, Snippet would bring her new foal for me to admire. She was such a beautiful creature; her coat shimmered in the sunlight, and I really had an infinity with this animal. I loved and adored her. Sometimes, if I was out riding and she was nearby, she would whinny and come running across to me. I made several offers to buy her, but the farmer would not sell.

It was many years later when I realised just how deep that infinity was.

Snippet is my animal spirit guide and animal soulmate, which explains why I feel such a strong bond with her. She has an aura that presents itself to me as a shimmering coat. Such an aura is attached only to highly evolved animals. She comes forward to me now in spirit form as a male unicorn called Sirius. It transpires that we have lived a few lives together, so we are evolving in parallel on a very high platform. It is obvious to me that animal communication is one of the gifts that is helping me to evolve.

Every year on Dartmoor, the pony drift occurs. This is when the guardians of the Dartmoor ponies round them up, sort out which ones should be returned to the moor, which ones are suitable for market, and which ones are to be shot. Snippet knew every year when this was happening, and she would come down to my yard. I was very naughty; I would hide her in the back of my stables with the other horses so that she could not be taken. In fact, on one occasion, she hid herself up on the moor, and the day after the pony drift happened, she appeared. Sadly, she disappeared one year, and I was not able to save her on that occasion.

I have been helping moorland ponies for over forty years and am sure that they will never cease to be important to me.

Mare is Taught a Lesson

Not long after I moved on to the moor, my neighbour, who lived at the end of the road that leads onto open moorland, popped in to voice her concerns about a mare that had been on her own for at least two weeks. She told me that the herd was on the other side of the bog and did not appear to want anything to do with her. I visited the area in question called Whiteworks. I stood and called on the matriarch of the herd, asking her to come and talk to me. At that time, I had recently had a knee operation and could not walk very far, so I asked that she come to me.

My husband, who had come along with me, was looking for the herd when a mare and foal trotted past him with a purpose. This was the matriarch of the herd, and she came right up to me and asked what was wrong. I told her about the isolated mare and asked if there was a problem. Apparently, the herd were teaching this young mare how to have some manners. They were keeping an eye on her and would invite her back into the herd when she had learned her lesson. The matriarch's foal was surprised to learn that

I could speak to the ponies; it was something that he had not come across before. I thanked the matriarch for her help, and they returned to the herd.

Foal Saved from Certain Death

One day, as I was driving towards Merrivale, I was asked for help. I stopped the car and wondered who had spoken to me. I got out of the car and walked along the road. It was early spring, and the snow was falling heavily. As I looked along the stone row, I spotted a mare who was giving birth to twin foals, a dangerous situation at any time of the year, but particularly perilous during such terrible weather. I stood back and watched because I didn't want to add to her stress. After the foals were born, I was horrified to witness her running at one of them and biting it on the neck. I could only assume that she didn't have enough strength to raise two foals at the same time and had chosen to kill one of them rather than let it starve to death. I ran up in tears, which made her walk away with the other foal. I was convinced that the foal she had attacked was dead, but I wrapped it up in my coat and started rubbing it. Suddenly it started to breathe again, and its eyes opened. I was so relieved.

I communicated to the foal and told it not to worry, I would look after it, and that is exactly what I did. I took it to my charity stables, and we brought it up. I also contacted the mare and told her that she had not killed her other foal, just stunned it. The foal grew into a happy pony, living a wonderful life with us at the charity. Another happy ending to what could have been a tragedy.

Pony Caught in Electrical Tape

Another day, I had a phone call from a walker who had been out with his dog on the Tavistock Golf Course. He was concerned about a pony he'd seen there. It appeared to have got tape around its rear leg at the fetlock. I went out to look for this lovely animal. The gorse bushes there are so high that you can walk past people and animals and not realise they are even there. There was a maze of little avenues through the bushes. Finally I just stopped at a junction of two paths. *This is crazy,* I thought. *I could be here all day looking for this pony.* I called upon the matriarch of the herd, and I sent her a vision of a pony with tape around its leg. She told me that she knew about the pony in question and that it was free now. I asked her what she meant, and she helped me to understand that the pony had got caught in the electrical tape that had been stretched around part of the golf course green. The pony had struggled and struggled until it had broken the tape. She was now free. However, there was some tape still wrapped around her fetlock, and it needed to be removed. The matriarch directed me to the pony, and I found it.

I called the farmer who owned the pony, and he came out with a helper. Between the three of us, we cut the tape off its leg. The tape was wrapped very tightly and was cutting into the pony's fetlock. We sprayed the injury with some blue antiseptic spray and released the foal. Another moorland pony helped!

Foal Rescued from Near Death

I had a phone call from some walkers who had been travelling across the moor at the top of Pork Hill near Tavistock. Whilst they were walking, they had seen a foal that seemed to be stuck in the bog. There was no herd nearby; in fact, there were no ponies at all for quite a distance, so they went into the bog and got the pony out. The foal followed them to the car park at the top of Pork Hill where they phoned me.

I went out with one of my trailers, collected the foal, and took it back to my yard. This foal owed its life to the lovely walkers who were only too pleased to be able to help.

Haven: Devastated by Loss of Guardian

A lady contacted me about a horse that was causing her some difficulties. I had been recommended to her by one of my previous clients. She was totally upfront and told me that she was very skeptical. She didn't believe in my work, but she was at her wits' end and didn't know where to turn. I was not surprised by her opinion; it is not unusual for guardians to see me as the last resort when they have problem animals. I asked her to send me a photograph of the horse along with its name. I would communicate with it.

In due course, the photograph of Haven arrived, and I opened the lines of communication with him. When I spoke to Haven, he repeatedly said,

'I killed her! I killed her!' His energy was so sad that I became very upset. I asked him to show me what had happened. The vision that he gave me was of a young girl dressed in her riding gear, jumping over a jump. As Haven went over the jump, the young girl came off and landed on the ground; she died immediately. Haven blamed himself for the accident and was as close to a nervous breakdown I have ever seen.

I asked him to let me help him. I discovered that he was still being ridden. He showed me a young man on his back using his legs and crop to make the horse move forward. Sadly, Haven was so deep in grief that the last thing he needed was someone on his back forcing him to do something he wasn't ready to do. This was a terrible way for him to be feeling, and it was dangerous for him to be ridden at that time. I told him I would ask the guardian to give him a break and allow him to recover from what had happened.

Before I could do this, I needed to know what had been happening at the yard and why Haven's guardian felt she needed my help. To help me understand, he gave me a vision of her arriving at the yard with a spirit girl (he didn't tell me if this was the young girl that died falling from his back.) I told him I would chat to his guardian about this as well. He also gave me some other messages for his guardian. When his guardian called, I was very careful with the information that I gave her. I explained about the spirit girl who came alongside her, and she confirmed that this was her daughter. When I told her that Haven blamed himself for her death, she was aghast and told me it had not been his fault; it had been an unfortunate accident. I also explained to the guardian that Haven needed time to recover from the death of her daughter. It would really help if he could be left alone for six weeks and not be ridden during this time. It would give him some time to grieve and recover. She agreed to this and thanked me for my help. She'd had various vets and animal behaviourists along to help Haven. She needed to be able to handle him and didn't want to have him put down as she didn't feel that he had done anything wrong. The guardian thanked me, and I told her to contact me if the issues continued. I would have been happy to talk to him again.

The following week, I received a telephone call from one of the stable girls at Haven's yard. She asked if I could speak to the guardian again, and of course I said yes. When she came on the phone, the first thing she did was apologise. Apparently she had given me a fake name because she didn't want me to go online and find any information about what had happened.

I assured her that I never use online searches; I always communicate with the animals and rely on messages they give me to pass on to their guardians, whether they are good or bad. She then went on to tell me that Haven had been a different horse during the last few days. She apologised for her skepticism and asked if she could contact me in six weeks so that I could make sure that he was ready to return to work. Of course, I agreed, and six weeks later, I communicated with Haven. He was fine. Another young lady wanted to ride him in competitions at a high level. I asked him if he was happy to do this, and he said he was. Haven eventually moved to another livery. He is now working with another young girl who is working her way through the competition levels. He is happy and relaxed, allowing his new guardians to ride him frequently.

Horse with a Second Chance

I was holding an animal communication workshop with about fifteen people at a livery yard. During the afternoon, we were going to do some communication with several horses in the yard. The first horse the guardians brought out was a problem horse, a cob. He stood there, and I introduced myself to him.

For the first time in my life, I heard a horse swear. He told me to fuck off! I was quite surprised. I asked all my pupils to stand back and give him lots of space as this animal was not in a good place. He appeared to be very angry. When speaking to animals, it is important to gain their permission to communicate. Communication can't be accomplished by force; animals must do it with their free will. I asked my pupils not to try and speak to him. I was concerned that, if I couldn't get to the bottom of the issue, he would end up being put to sleep.

I turned to the cob and apologised for anything the humans may have done to him to make him so angry. I told him that animal abusers are rare, and that there are far more guardians who are kind, loving, and caring. I assured him that everyone around him now was just that. I told him we would like to offer him some healing. He was very concerned that we would touch him, so I assured him that we did not need to touch him, but that he needed to relax, not to kick out. I didn't want him to hurt us. He agreed to let us help him, so we went through the process of asking and answering questions.

This cob had come from Ireland. The reason he hated humans was that he had been hobbled, a process of tying a horse's legs together so it is unable to move. Some believe it can induce calm in an animal. This cob had been hobbled and tied to a very thick post and just left to fight it out. As a result of this, the horse had been stressed, fearful, and very angry. This is not the way to break a horse in. 'Breaking,' despite what the word implies, must be done with love and tenderness; it shouldn't be done with fear. We continued helping this beautiful animal with a group healing session. It is very important to be honest with animals. They are not fools, and horses in particular are extremely sensitive. With this in mind, I showed him the consequences of his actions.

I told him that he needed to forgive and forget. He needed to move on because the young girl who was his new owner had bought him from a dealer who had been planning to send him to be slaughtered. She had saved him from death, and all he was doing was being nasty to everyone who walked past the stable. He had been turning his back on everyone and kicking out. He'd also had a go at her with his teeth. I told him that his behaviour was not acceptable. All the young girl wanted to do was to look after him and one day be able to ride him. He needed to treat her with the respect she deserved and not allow his previous experiences in Ireland to taint the life he could have in the future.

We left the livery after the healing session was finished. Three months later, I heard that the young girl was riding him and that he was a completely different animal.

Energy Reset Saves Horse

I received a phone call from the head groom who managed a yard for a hunt in another part of the country. (Here I must say that I don't agree with hunting or any form of animal sport.) She said that they had bought a large cob, around fifteen hands, a few months earlier. He was called Barney. She told me that he was a nasty horse who bit, charged, and kicked. He wouldn't let anyone near him, and if they managed somehow to get on his back, he would throw them off, resulting in a hurt rider. I said I would try to help, and they sent me a photograph.

When I entered the horse's energy and asked for permission to talk to him, the first thing he said was, 'What is the matter with you humans? I've had so many names; every new guardian gives me a different name. Why?' I explained to him that humans are strange creatures. We like to choose the names of our animals. I suggested that he had been to lots of different homes. He had not settled anywhere and probably had been playing up wherever he was. He agreed with me, and I asked him what his birth mother had called him. He gave me a name, and I told him I would pass that information on to his new guardian. This was the name that he would like to be used.

I then asked him if he would let me help him. I wanted to know why he was being so nasty to his new guardians. He revealed that he had also come from Ireland, and he had been hobbled just like the previous animal, but he had also been castrated without any sedation. They had not used a vet because they felt they were experienced enough to do the procedure themselves. I was very shocked that such treatment existed. I knew that humans were capable of some awful things, but this was just terrible. He also showed me being in the lorry on the boat crossing over the sea. He didn't like the feeling, and he had felt dreadfully poorly. I apologised for the treatment he had received and told him that the humans that ran the hunting yard would look after him, feed him, and exercise him. However, again, I had to explain the consequences of his behaviour and how they had bought him expecting to be able to ride him. He had already hurt one human, and if he continued to behave that way, then they would have no qualms in having him shot dead.

I asked him to forgive and forget and to allow them to catch him, to tack him up, and to ride him. I explained that, if he allowed them to do all these things, he would get the best of care. He listened intently and then confirmed that he would allow these new guardians to look after him. I told him that I would relay his information to the guardians and that it was up to him from now on.

After speaking to Barney, I rang the head groom and told her what I had found out. I also mentioned his true name and explained that he had not been responding because he didn't like the name Barney. She agreed that they would use his 'real' name. I also suggested that she contact me before anyone attempted to ride him so that I could forewarn him. She agreed. Around ten o'clock that very evening, she rang me to say that the master of the hunt had told her that, if they didn't ride the 'bloody' horse the following day, then he would be shot. I communicated with the horse again and told him that he would have to be groomed, tacked up, and ridden the next day. If there were any problems—^bucking a rider off or otherwise playing up, then he would be shot when they got back to the yard. The following morning, I received a phone call from the head groom, who told me that Barney had been an absolute gem. He had behaved and received many compliments about his behaviour. I was so proud of him because it cannot have been easy to eat humble pie with so much hate and anger from his previous experiences.

About nine months later, I received a phone call from the head groom again. She told me that Barney had put a girl in hospital after she attempted to clip him out as she got him ready for hunting. I told the girl that she should have asked me to communicate with him again. The clippers would have triggered the memory of the brutal castration that he had experienced, and I was not surprised that he had lashed out. I re-entered his energy and explained to him that they were only clipping his coat so that, when he was hunting, he wouldn't sweat and lose condition. I told him that they would do that from time to time, but that they would not hurt him. Hopefully Barney learned to trust his new guardians and have a lovely life.

Ex Racehorse Revitalised After Energy Assistance

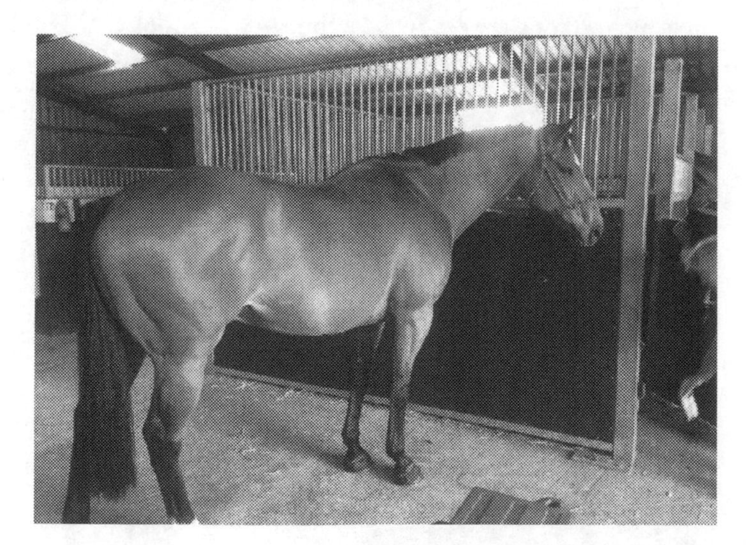

I had to go to a yard near Cirencester, a long way from my home, to treat Brandy, a four-year-old ex-racehorse who had raced on the flat. The gentleman who owned Brandy had bought him because he wasn't doing very well on the race circuit. He told me that, at times, this horse would be unsound and very unbalanced. The vets were unable to find a cause and just couldn't get to the bottom of it. The guardian was finding that he had to rest Brandy every time he rode him. He asked if I would communicate with Brandy, which I did.

The man had never used an animal communicator before and was rather intrigued-not skeptical, just intrigued. I went into the stable and told the gentleman that I needed peace and quiet when I was communicating. I promised I would relay any information after I had spoken to Brandy. I tuned into Brandy's energy, and he showed me a vision of him on the gallops running flat out. But the next minute he was on the ground, the jockey was off, and Brandy had hurt himself. Since that accident, he had not been right. He showed me his leg, which needed to be rested often.

After I listened to this story and received a few other messages, I told the guardian that I needed to adjust Brandy's energy because it was all over the place; it was no wonder that Brandy was not balanced. This had been caused by the trauma of a fall. Without touching Brandy, I stood fairly close to him and readjusted his entire body from the top of his head, down over his neck, along his withers, and along his back right to his rear end. I then said to the guardian, 'I have readjusted him; I have done some healing on him, and for the next twenty-four hours, his physical body will need to adjust to the energy shift. He may have an upset tummy. He may drink lots of water, which is the body's way of eliminating itself of toxins.'

After I treated Brandy, his guardian asked me to look at a little Shetland pony called Sammy. This pony had a large lump under his chin, and there was some blood coming down his nose. The guardian said he had been like that for quite a while. They had called several vets; they were all baffled, and they couldn't get to the bottom of it. I agreed to communicate with Sammy. I discovered there was a trauma energy hanging around. Energy can affect the physical body, and this is why doctors and vets can't understand the work I do.

To enable the body to self-heal, the energy needs to flow correctly. The lump that had appeared was the only way the physical body could deal with the trauma. I conducted some healing on little Sammy, again not touching him. I evened his energy out and helped him with any questions and queries he had. I was able to relay some information to the guardian that Sammy wanted him to know. After doing the healing, I was given a nice cup of tea before I left.

Several months later, I received information from the guardian about Brandy the thoroughbred and Sammy the Shetland pony. Brandy, as I had predicted, had drunk a huge amount of water-the guardian could not believe how much and within ten days, he was sound. The lump on Sammy gradually went down and finally disappeared, and the bleeding stopped. The pony wasn't so grumpy and became much friendlier. So, my visit was well worthwhile. I was able to help two animals with energy issues and improve their quality of life.

Introduction to Zimbabwe

This is a story about communicating with a human spirit, however it serves as an introduction to the next horse communication story.

I worked for a lovely family company in Cornwall for over twenty years as a salesperson. During this time, they were not aware that I was an animal communicator; however, one day whilst I was travelling to see my own horses, my husband, who was reading the *Western Morning News,* stumbled upon a two-page feature with photographs about a serviceman who had died in Afghanistan. I happened to glance across as I was driving, and I began thinking how sad it was that all those men had died. Tears started rolling down my face. I heard a human voice say, 'Yes, it is so sad, and I was not able to say goodbye to my family. I am so upset.' I asked the young serviceman if he was still on this planet. Had he not crossed over into the light? He told me he hadn't. I told him that he was in a dangerous place. As I was driving, I asked him to go. I would stop the car, and I would call him forward again when I got down to my horses.

When we arrived, I left my husband to see to the horses. I sat on a bale of straw, and I called this young serviceman forward. I told him it was very dangerous where he was if he hadn't gone into the light, which he hadn't. I told him that I was going to call down the light, and the angels would be there. He needed to step into the light, and then he would cross over and be with his family members on the other side. He said he would, but before he went, he wanted to give his parents a message through me, and he wanted them to receive the message after he walked into the light and crossed over.

I didn't think any more about it until I got to work. I sat in the office with my boss, Martin, and I suddenly found myself telling him about the work I do, the animal communication, and then I started talking about this serviceman coming forward. I told him how I had called the light down and how he had stepped into the light. I told him that I didn't know how I was going to get the message to his parents because I had no idea who they were. But I should have had more trust in the archangels and the higher realm. There is no such a thing as coincidence; there's always a reason for everything. Martin was sitting in the chair, hands behind his head, twirling in his seat and smiling. I finished telling him the story about this serviceman, and I looked at him. I said, 'You don't believe a bloody word I've said, do you?'

He laughed and said, 'No, no. Let me tell you why I'm smiling, Maureen.' He told me that his family members had gone to a remembrance service for that very soldier who was the son of a friend of theirs. He hadn't gone because someone needed to stay with the business. I expressed my sympathy and asked if Martin would get the message to the serviceman's parents. Of course he said he would. I don't know why I was amazed; you could have knocked me off the seat with a feather. That opened a door to other opportunities because my employers then knew that I do animal communication and other spiritual things.

Zimbabwe: Nonstarter to Winner

One day, whilst I was talking to Martin on the phone, his father chipped into the conversation and asked if I could communicate with his racehorse who wouldn't race. I told Martin to get Russell to send me a photograph and the name of the horse, and I would see if I could find out what the problem was.

When I received the photograph, I found a quiet place and communicated with the horse, who was called Zimbabwe. He was a beautiful creature, but his energy was jumping all over the place; he was very excited. I asked Zimbabwe if this was how he felt most of the time, and he said it was. I asked him if we could do a race together over the hurdles so that I could pick up what was happening. I placed my energy on his back to experience what was happening. He agreed, but he just danced on the spot and didn't move forward. I worked out that he was experiencing the equivalent of the sort of stage fright a human might have, the adrenaline rush was seizing up his body.

I told Zimbabwe that I would teach him how to control it. As we began to race, I showed him how to control his breathing, when to step out, how far out to go before he jumped.

When the session finished, I told Russell what the problem was and told him that I had shown Zimbabwe how to cope with his condition. Hopefully, at his next race in Exeter, he would be okay. I went along with Zimbabwe for his race in Exeter and stayed with his energy. Whilst sitting in my car, using my ability, I was able to be the jockey by placing my energy on Zimbabwe's back. I stayed with him throughout the race. I could see the entire race from the back of this beautiful animal, the horses running beside us, a jockey falling off and we won! Previously Zimbabwe had become a bit of an embarrassment because he wouldn't actually race; he'd just prance about on the spot. Russell was so thrilled that Zimbabwe had won, he pulled me into the guardian's ring and said, 'You have got to come in! How wonderful.' Zimbabwe raced many times after that, and he always finished in the top three. He conquered his stage fright and eventually learned the ability to control that adrenaline rush, so I wasn't needed to accompany him racing anymore. Fantastic! He was another horse I helped.

Healing Saves Pony from Operation

My charity, South West Equine Protection, had helped nearly four hundred animals by the time I handed the reins over to the Mare and Foal Sanctuary. One particular case that sticks in my mind concerned a Shetland pony called Lucy. She was out on loan with a lovely spiritual family down in Cornwall. They phoned me and asked me to come down and look at her because a small lump had developed on her muzzle, and the vets couldn't figure out a cause or how to treat it. The vets wanted to sedate Lucy to do some tests on her, but the family didn't want to do that, so they asked me to communicate with her and do some healing. I often work with a crystal wand, which the spirits and angels guided me to buy from a shop in Glastonbury. It cost several hundred pounds, but I couldn't pass it by; I had to buy it. I went down to Cornwall with my wand and looked at the lump on Lucy's muzzle. Whilst I was working on her, the gentleman there said, 'I can see a purple light coming from your wand.' I told him that it was the healing power that was working on the lump. After I had completed my session with Lucy and had a lovely cup of tea, I headed home. At the end of that week, I heard from the guardian, who had taken photographs daily throughout the week. The lump had got gradually smaller and smaller, and by the end of the week, it had disappeared.

Deceased Pony Unaware it had Passed

On another occasion I was asked to communicate with a pony that had gone missing from his field. He was a black pony, and when I got into his energy, I asked him where he was. He told me that he wasn't missing. He was there, but his guardian wasn't feeding him. I asked him if he could show me where he was. His vision showed me a fast-flowing, wide river that had flooded his field and washed him away.

I told him that he was dead, which he didn't believe to begin with. Because of the trauma he had experienced, he had not realised that he had died. I could see his body further down the river. He had died, but he had not crossed over into the light, which was why he could see his guardian coming to see him but not feed him. I told him that, if he let me bring the light down and call the archangels forward, they would help him cross over. This is what I did, and he was able to join his spirit family.

I phoned the guardian but was rather disappointed by her reaction. When I told her that her pony had been swept away by the floods and drowned further down the river, her response was very cold. However, it was her animal, and it was her right to deal with the situation how she felt.

Horse Communicates Through his Mother to Me

A lady contacted me to ask me to talk to her six horses. One of these horses was male, but the energy that I was talking to was female, which was slightly confusing. This female was very angry and fed up. She wanted to come back because she was very unhappy where she was. I tried to assure her and then did some healing on her, but I was still baffled because the photograph was of a male horse who had a male name, but I was certainly speaking to a female.

When I spoke to the guardian, I gave her the messages from all the horses. When I started giving her the message from the final horse, she stopped me and remarked, 'Maureen, it's a male!' I agreed with her, but I confirmed that the energy I had spoken to was definitely female. Partway through the message, the lady said that she realised that I had been talking to the male's mother. She had been sold a little while earlier. It appeared that this horse had allowed me to speak to his mum through him because she was so unhappy. I told the guardian that the female would be coming back soon. Within a week, the guardian rang me and said that the people who had bought the mare were bringing her back. I had never before experienced an animal allowing another animal to talk to me through his energy.

As I have mentioned, I have communicated with animals all my life (over forty years.) No one understood what I did; I was always known as 'that weird girl'. Because of this, I stopped talking about it openly but continued to communicate with animals in secret. The animals knew that I could talk to them, but the humans had no idea, I am sad to say.

I often have to apologise for humans to the animals that I help. Humans seem to think that life is all about what they want and not about whether that is right for the animals. In this world, we have become use to things being instant; humans want everything immediately. People don't stop to think about what they are doing. Animals are far more sensitive. They are not machines; they have feelings and souls, and their reactions and instincts are far quicker than ours. When are we going to understand we are not superior? Animals are far superior to us. They are more caring, more loving, and more understanding. They would not do the kinds of uncaring things we do. I have helped many animals, more than I can remember. I'm not sure where this gift comes from other than it comes from above. I know I work with the archangels and the seventh realm; I work with some very high ascended masters, and I have worked with Jesus and Mother Mary. I never truly know what is going to happen when I am doing an animal communication, who is going to come through and work through my body and who is going to be there to help me. I never question what happens; I always accept that what I do will work, but it gives me such great pleasure to be able to see all this happening without the use of drugs. All it takes is just love, energy, and healing. I am so thrilled to be an animal communicator; it gives me such joy.

Celestial Guidance: Pony and Two Foals

I was heading off to a horse show when my husband phoned me and asked me to return home. He said that a mare had unexpectedly turned up outside my house with her brand-new foal along with her yearling. They were all standing by our cars when, with no warning, the mare dropped down dead leaving the yearling and foal beside her oblivious to what had just happened. I immediately turned around and drove back home.

I found the farmer who owned the mare, and he came and took her carcass away, telling me that I could take in the yearling and new-born foal, which was actually only a few days old.

As founders of the South West Equine Protection, we took them into our care and looked after them. This was one of the occasions when the archangels guided animals to me that needed my help. The mare knew instinctively she had to get to my house because she was dying and needed her foals to be safe and cared for. The angels in their divine wisdom had guided her to me so I could help her. It was such an honour to help this animal, especially when she knew she was going to die, bless her. I believe there had obviously been some complications with the birth of the foal; she probably hadn't cleansed properly and had died of septicaemia.

I thanked the archangels for guiding the mare to me so that the foals could survive, and we were able to bring them up. The farmer would have more than likely put the foals down as he did not have the time to feed them every few hours. They were welcomed into our yard and well looked after. They turned into lovely ponies, and it was a pleasure to have them.

Pony Saved with Angelic Healing

Another pony I have helped was suffering with laminitis. The guardian wanted me to do some healing. Laminitis is a condition connected with the hooves; it is the *laminae* within the hoof that is affected. Usually this is caused by the animal being overweight; sometimes it is caused by pressure shock from over working on hard ground. Other times, actually more often than not, it is caused by too much rich grass that contains high levels of protein.

I arranged to go up and visit the lovely little Shetland pony, whose name was Dougal. He was very much a character, and his laminitis was very bad. The laminae was in trouble, and the pedal bone in the bottom of the hoof was also compromised. The pedal bone takes the pressure of the body when the horse lands; unfortunately, this bone in Dougal's hoof had rotated. The rotation was extremely painful because this part of the hoof is incredibly sensitive. This indicated to me severe laminitis, and I was all too aware that the vets usually recommend that animals in this state are put down.

On visiting Dougal, I realised, via communication, the level of pain he was experiencing. The guardian had previously asked the farrier and vet to see Dougal, and they had been giving him painkillers, so he was not in as much pain as he could have been. I performed a healing on Dougal, which was a lot of hard work. I used my wand, which enabled me to get very deep into the animal's body. I also went inside his mind and did a psychic operation, which I am able to do with the archangels guiding me as always. The archangels and I did a lot of work on this dear pony's hooves, and when I finished, I told the guardian that Dougal might well be in a lot of pain for the next twenty-four hours. This was because the pedal bone was going to rotate back to the original position. I told the guardian not to panic; once it had fully rotated, the pony would feel so much better.

I left, and a few days later, the guardian called to tell me that Dougal was eighty percent better. His attitude was back, he was frisking her for treats, she had taken him for short walks (he could not walk easily before), and he even broke into a trot on one occasion, which was wonderful.

Six weeks later, the farrier could not find any sign of laminitis at all, so not only had the pedal bone rotated back into position, but the laminae had managed to repair itself too. The guardian was absolutely thrilled to bits because, without my help, the animal would have had to be put down. Dougal had a lot to say about this.

I am not saying that the archangels and I can work this magic every time, but it really does depend on where the animals are on their soul journey. Just like humans, animals have a soul journey. If it is destined that an animal is to be put down, I can't alter that. When I do my healing, I have trust and faith that it will work. When healing doesn't work, it is because humans block it; they, as well as animals, have free will. Animals do not block me because they are far more accepting of the work I do. They believe in the help I can give with the archangels working through me.

Whether I am doing healing on an animal or a human, I accept that my efforts will work. It will be unsuccessful only if the healing powers are blocked through resistance.

Horse in Spirit Guiding his Earthbound Guardian

Beau - Horse - Heart Field

The next horse that I helped was a horse called Beau, who had been deceased for three to four years. The lady who had owned him was still grieving over his death; she obviously had a very strong bond and connection with him.

She asked if I could communicate with him and relay how much she missed and loved him. I was happy to communicate with Beau for her. I tuned into Beau's energy, and he came forward and gave me messages for her. He showed me a vision: several strands of grass shaped into a heart with the seed heads in the middle of the heart joining at the bottom. He told me to tell her that this would be significant when she was looking for some stables and a yard to rent. I gave her this message and told her that Beau would be with her when she saw this sign, which I described to her. I told her it was very significant, and she would feel him with her at the appropriate time.

I heard nothing from her for quite a while, but then she sent me a photograph by email. She rang me and said, 'I have been looking everywhere for a new yard to rent. Every time I thought I had found the perfect yard, I couldn't finalise the deal. Then one day something made me stop near a cottage. I went in and asked if the yard and fields were available to rent. I now have my new yard. It is in Criller Mill just inside the Cornish border.' The story doesn't end there. She told me she went to visit her mum in Wales. Her mother said to her, 'I still have the saddle, bridle, and everything that belonged to Beau.' She told her mum that she would take it back to her new yard at Criller Mill. While still in Wales, she got talking to a young man, and he asked where she came from. She told him she lived between Tavistock and Callington. He told her that was where he came from and that his parents still lived in an area called Criller Mill. She told him that she had just started renting a yard in Criller Mill, and it turned out that it was his mum and dad's property. The man said, 'Have you looked at aerial views of the fields online?' When she said no, he replied, 'Well, you should search the Internet. One of the fields is heart shaped.' She was over the moon—her reading from Beau had come true. Beau was with her, and she was taking his bridle and saddle to the new yard. Obviously, he was the one with the angels who had helped her and guided her to knock on the door of the house and find out about the yard. As I said earlier, there are no such things as coincidences!

I have worked with thousands and thousands of horses, dogs, and cats, far too many for me to remember. I don't always hear back from the guardians to learn how well the reading worked. Very often, the only time I learn about positive results is when someone recommends me to the owner of another animal that is in some sort of distress.

I have also helped lizards, snakes, and other reptiles, communicating with ease to all of them. Once I communicated with a lady's two dragons. The energy was fantastic, so different. It is nice for me to experience all energies and to get the feeling for different animals and birds on our planet.

It is not unusual for animals to come to me out of the blue. I have kept bird feeders for years. My husband could not believe what happened one day when I went outside to hang a bell-shaped suet and seed ball. As I was standing there holding the bell, a blue tit landed right on my hand, and we had a lovely conversation. Spirits send birds as messengers very often, and this was one of them. My husband took a photograph of me and the bird. It was a fantastic experience.

On another occasion, we went to Glastonbury and visited the famous well. As I sat on the seat by the head of the well meditating, something spoke to me. I opened my eyes to see a robin perched on my arm. He said, 'I have been sent to give you messages.' He gave me a message from my spirit family (my mum), but also from the angels. When the robin had finished with his message, I thanked him warmly, and he took off.

The angels and spirits send animals to me frequently. On another occasion when I was getting ready to go out for my birthday, I had the window open, and a robin landed on the sill and said to me, 'I am bringing you happy birthday wishes from your family, from your mum, dad, brothers, and sisters on the spirit side.' I thanked him, and he flew off.

Why do humans shut all of this off? There is all this wonder around us that provides many opportunities for us to bond with nature. We are all born with our brains wide open and ready to communicate with animals; sadly, our brains gradually close when we are told not to be stupid. We can't believe in things like that sort of communication because it cannot be expressed in terms of black and white. Somehow, if we can't see it, it doesn't exist. But this is not true, completely not true! There is so much communication going on. When I hold my animal communication workshops, I teach people who are extreme novices. Once I have guided them through various meditations, reintroducing their brains to becoming open, they are able to communicate with animals in varying degrees. One of the best students I ever met didn't intend to come to the workshop; he had driven someone there and decided to stay. He turned out to be one of the best animal communicators I have ever trained, and he couldn't believe it himself. So, we can all do this! We were born to do this, but it has been shut off due to the beliefs of the society that we live in. I believe we have been brainwashed to believe only in phenomena that can be proved scientifically and nothing else. If we don't use the senses we have been given, we are heading towards a great global failure. We are doing so much damage to humans, animals, the land, and the seas. We would not be doing this if we used that part of our brains. We must be more conscious, more compassionate, more loving and caring.

Next, I am going to talk about a few of the dogs I have communicated with over the years.

Dog Communication Stories

An Entity Draining the Life Force Out of Rossi

Rossi

Rossi had been ill for three years, and his guardians had taken him to various vets as well as to several alternative practitioners. Rossi's guardian had got very upset on her last visit as the vet said the dog had only a few weeks to live. She loved this animal to bits and was devastated. She had spent a small fortune to try to help dear Rossi.

Rossi's guardian came to me because, while walking Rossi on the beach, she had spoken with a friend of mine who suggested that she get in touch. She rang and asked if I could help. I told her that I couldn't promise anything, but I would try. I asked for a photograph so that I could communicate with him.

At this time, they lived down in the southern region of Cornwall. As soon as I got into Rossi's energy, I was very aware of an evil presence. I quickly came out of the energy because I didn't want that entity to attach itself to me. As much as I protect myself, I still have the fear of negative energy getting into my very high and very sensitive energy. When I released myself out of Rossi's energy, he showed me what was attached to him, and he told me he didn't like it. I phoned my friend and asked her, 'Can you tell me if these people are open? Because I am going to have to talk to them about things that may make them think I am bonkers.'

She said, 'The woman is okay, but her husband is very skeptical.' I needed to do something because this entity was sucking the energy and life out of Rossi.

Rossi was not ill; he was being plagued by the entity. I relayed my findings to my friend, 'I need to go down to their home to cleanse this energy and take it to the light, but also to cleanse the people that live there, their home, and their vehicles. It would be no good for me to cleanse only the wife, the house, and her car. I must be sure to cleanse the husband and his car; otherwise, I'll be wasting my time. If I don't send everything to the light, the entity can re-manifest and rebuild the energy to continue doing what it has been doing.'

My friend got the lady to ring me, and I relayed this information to her; however, she explained that her husband was not keen. I told her that I would not come down, and unfortunately Rossi would suffer. She reconsidered, had a word with her husband, and rang me back, ensuring his full cooperation. As soon as I arrived at the house, the dog came up to me and sat on my feet. Hs guardians were surprised because, as they had told me, Rossi never went to anyone. I told them that Rossi knew that I had gone there to help him. I told Rossi that I would send whatever it was to the light, and I explained the procedure to the woman's husband.

I started the cleansing. Near the end of the process, the entity appeared, I could see it! As always, I had gone prepared and had four archangels with me. We got the entity into the light, and the archangels helped me with the cleansing of the house, the people in it, and everything connected to it.

When it was all over, Rossi climbed into his bed and fell fast asleep. Understandably he was exhausted because the entity had taken all his energy; he needed to rest up and repair himself. Normally, his guardians had been carrying Rossi out to urinate; however, within an hour, he took himself out into the garden. I had told them there were things that could happen due to the length of time the entity had been with them. Rossi could be sick. He might have the runs. He might drink lots of water. He might basically appear worse for the next twenty-four hours.

But Rossi fortunately showed only signs of being a lot better, even though he did drink a lot of water. This communication was done two years ago, and Rossi is still alive. He did not need any operations as suggested by the vet. The entity had been sucking the life out of him. Now the husband and his wife have gone from being very skeptical to saying to people, 'If it wasn't for Maureen, Rossi would be dead. We can't thank her enough.'

Bailey Healed by Eye of Horus

Bailey

Bailey was a beautiful dog who had health issues; his guardian had already spent a fortune on vet services, but to no avail. I was at the guardian's home one day, and she asked me to do some healing on her dog.

I opened myself up and called on the archangels, my guides, as well and others in the higher realm who work through me or with me. As I have mentioned before, various deities, ascended masters, and energies work through me. So, I opened up and invited them in for the greater good of Bailey and myself. Whenever I am doing healing, I close my eyes, concentrate, and put the energy where I want it to go within the body of the animal or human I am working on. Usually the energy is different in each animal or person I am working on. I find sometimes it can be hot, cold, tingly, or like fire; it can be many things. However, that day it was different. That energy was something I had not experienced before. As I closed my eyes and concentrated, I felt as if there were electric sparks emanating out of my fingers, and my thumbs on both hands were pulsating; I could feel them expanding and contracting as my eyes were firmly closed.

I did the healing on Bailey while his guardian sat on the floor beside him. Once I had finished, I opened my eyes to see that the guardian's jaw was almost touching the ground; the look on her face indicated she was almost petrified. I asked her, 'What's the matter?'

She said, 'Maureen, that was really weird. If I hadn't seen it with my own eyes, I wouldn't have believed it.' When I asked her what had happened, she replied, 'Your thumbs were pulsating! They were expanding and contracting!'

I said with excitement, 'Yes, I could feel a different energy going through my hands.'

She then said, 'Yes, but what is even more strange, Maureen, is that an eye appeared at the base of your left thumb. I couldn't believe it!'

I hastily replied, 'Why didn't you shake me so I could see it as well? I could sense the sensations that were happening, but I didn't know anything about the eye!'

'Maureen,' she said, 'If I hadn't seen it with my own eyes, I never would have believed it.'

A few days later, she sent me a drawing of exactly what she had seen. It was the eye of Horus. Horus was one of the most significant Egyptian gods. The eye of Horus is a symbol that represents protection and healing. I never know who is going to work with me to help me to heal animals. Bailey, needless to say, was a lot better for quite a while after that session.

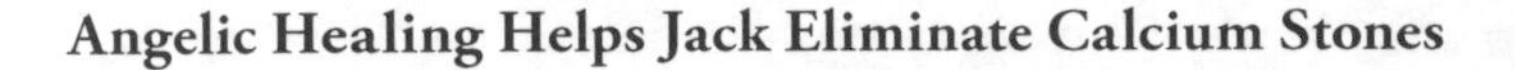

Angelic Healing Helps Jack Eliminate Calcium Stones

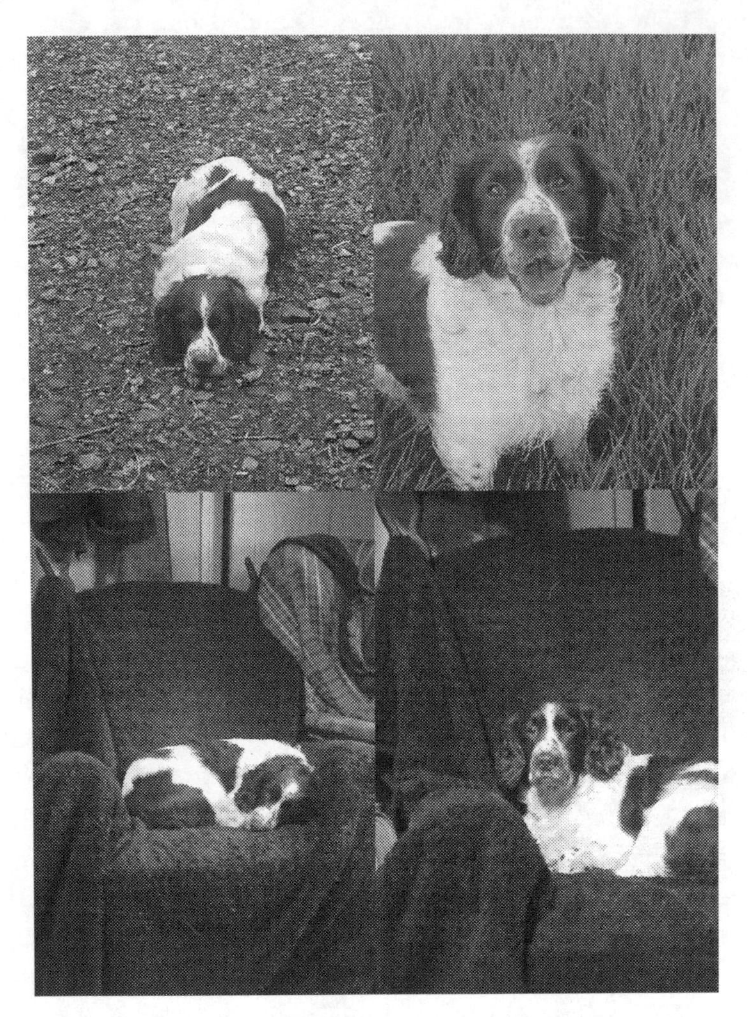

The guardian of a lovely spaniel called Jack rang me and said, 'I met you at one of the psychic fairs, and I am wondering if you could help my dog.' I asked him what was wrong. He said, 'We have been back and forth at the vets' office, and I have spent a fortune so far. He is struggling to urinate, and they just don't know what's wrong. They want to sedate him and do some tests.' He continued, 'I am now getting fed up and have lost confidence in the vets. I really get the feeling that, for them, it's more about money than it is about my dog. I am not happy with the vets, and I wondered if you would communicate with him.' I told him I would.

When I connected with the dog, oh boy, did I feel all that was going on. I asked the dog what was wrong, and he replied, 'I am having awful trouble. I can't pee. I have excruciating pain; in fact, it is so painful that I don't want to talk.' I told him that it was fine. I told him I would do some healing on him, and I asked his permission to do a psychic operation. He said it would be okay.

I did a psychic operation on him with the archangels assisting. When we got inside Jack, we could see that everything was extremely red and inflamed, and I could see a build-up of tiny little calcium bits. He was having trouble urinating because this was blocking the passage. The archangels and I blasted the calcium bits all away. Before this, I had thought he had swallowed stones that had caused the problem. When I completed the healing, I rang the guardian and said, 'Your dog may well be in a lot of pain for the next twenty-four hours, and I mean really bad pain. Be aware of that. We have done a psychic operation, and there were stones; however, they may be calcium stones rather than stones that he swallowed. We have blasted them and broken them up, and he will need to pass them, so he may well yelp as he is peeing. After the passing, Jack should feel a lot better.'

Within an hour, the dog went outside, and the man rang me and said, 'Jack has just had the longest pee I have ever seen him do! It's a real puddle, and I am so happy and so relieved that he is able to relieve himself.' He also told me that, after Jack had peed, he had run around in excitement. I told him that all would be fine. As time went by, his waterworks all got back to normal. The young guardian came to see me at the next Mind Body Spirit Fair and couldn't thank me enough.

Missing Dog Located and Reunited with Anxious Guardians

Late one Sunday evening, a friend phoned and told me she had been out to take her dog for a walk on Kitt Hill, an area just inside Cornwall near Callington. Along the way, she had seen a poster about a lost spaniel called Louis. The dog had been lost for about a week. My friend said, 'My heart has gone out to him. I just feel sorry for the dog. I thought of you and thought if anyone can find Louis, it would be you.' I thanked her and asked her if she could describe Louis. My friend told me he was brown and white, and she gave me the name and telephone number of the guardian. I started to tune into Louis without a photograph. I have done this a few times; however, I prefer to have a picture if I can so that I know I have made a connection with the right animal.

When I turned into Louis, I could see him walking down the track from Kitt Hill. His tongue was hanging out, and as soon as he came up close to me, I just found myself in tears. I asked him, 'What's the matter? Why are we up here?'

Louis replied, 'I am lost!' I responded, saying, 'Yes, I know, Louis. That's why I am talking to you. I want to try to get you back to your guardians, but first, why did you run off?'

He said, 'I was picking up on the scent of rabbits and various other things, and I just wandered off. Then I realised I had gone too far and couldn't find my way back.'

I told him, 'Louis, all will be okay. Where are you now?' I then explained, 'I am attaching a lead to you, an energetic leash in the etheric sense. So take me to where you are now.'

We went over boulders and hedges and through bracken for a few miles before we stopped. Louis said, 'This is where I am.' He then gave me a vision of the location. I could see a bay horse in a nearby field, a white cottage, and a green galvanised barn. I asked him if that was where he was now, and he said it was. I informed him I was going to ask his guardians to come and collect him; however, it would probably be the next day, as we were communicating late at night. I also told him to sit and stay right where he was because I might never be able to find him again if he moved. Louis assured me that he would stay, but he told me that he was frightened. I asked what he was frightened of, and he gave me visions of lightning and thunder. I explained that we had had a thunderstorm the night before and asked if it had hurt him. He said it hadn't. I then asked him if it was happening now, and he said it wasn't. I then told him, 'Please don't be frightened. Stay there, and I will get your guardians to come and pick you up in the morning.' With that, I disconnected from him and rang the guardians.

Please bear in mind they had no idea who I was or the type of work I do.

They didn't know me at all. And this was all happening around 9.30 on a Sunday evening. When the lady answered, I said, 'Please be patient and listen to me. I have located Louis for you. I am an animal communicator.'

She said, 'Oh dear.' When I asked her what was wrong, she said, 'I'm a Christian.'

I replied, 'Sweetheart, I work with the archangels. Is there anything better than that? And besides, I know where Louis is. Whether you believe me or not, it really doesn't matter. Isn't it worth checking out if there is a possibility that Louis is there?' She apologised, and I described what road to go down to look for a white cottage, a green galvanised barn, and a bay horse in the field. I told her that Louis would be waiting there for her. She listened and fully understood.

The next day, I was a monitor at a local pony market amongst other things, so I was not at home to receive her call. When I finally arrived home, I rang her and asked if she had found Louis. 'Well,' she said, 'my husband is very skeptical and has refused to go and look.' I told her that she had nothing to lose by looking. She told me that they had spent all day putting up posters around Callington. I informed her that that area was in the wrong one, and she agreed. The lady said she finally begged her husband to take her down the road that I told her about and just try to see if Louis was there. They drove down the road and saw the green galvanised barn and the white cottage. And right there, they spotted Louis in the middle of the field. She said, 'We got out and called him, but he wouldn't come, so we had to go and pick him up.' Louis was very dehydrated, so they had taken him to the vet, who put him on a saline drip. Luckily, the vet said Louis would be fine. I told her how pleased I was and she couldn't thank me enough.

Not long after that, I had a phone call from someone at a magazine called *Take a Break*. The reporter had picked up on this story and had asked the guardian if they could publish Louis's story. Louis's guardian gave them permission. The reporter asked me if I could attend the interview with Louis's guardian. We all arranged to meet up at Kit Hill where Louis first went missing.

I was listening to the guardian describe how Louis had gone missing. She described the trauma they had gone through for a week or so. The *Take a Break* reporter took photographs. As the guardian spoke to the reporter, I heard her say that her husband just would not believe all of this even though they had Louis back; in fact, the day after they found Louis, on his way home from work, he had knocked on the cottage door to asked to speak to Maureen Rolls. The lady said, 'I am sorry. I don't know that person.'

He explained what had happened. He then said to her, 'What I can't understand is why you didn't think it was strange to have a dog sitting in the middle of your field.'

She responded, 'My neighbour a few fields away has two brown-and-white spaniels that look like Louis.'

He continued, 'There is another thing I don't understand. Maureen said white cottage, green galvanised barn, and a bay horse in the field. There was no horse in the field.'

'No,' she said, 'I moved the horse into another field yesterday.' So, she had moved the horse before they got there.

The husband was still very skeptical. He still thought I had fabricated the whole thing, but the bay horse was in the field at the time of my communication. I did have a little bit of a giggle to myself and thought, *Oh boy, what does it take to get some people to realise that you can communicate with animals, and they do talk to us.* In fact, they talk to their guardians all the time. Animals communicate telepathically and with body language, just as we humans do. Communication doesn't come only from our open mouths.

Located Missing Dog After Cliff Fall

A dog had got lost in North Devon. The family had come down from Oxfordshire and were spending a bank holiday weekend in a cottage they usually visited. They decided to go for a coastal walk along the cliffs in Coombe Martin near Ilfracombe. The cliffs are horrendously high with a sheer drop to the sea. Nevertheless, they all happily walked along the path chatting among themselves. When they had walked enough, they all sat down for a tea break and realised that the dog was missing. They spent the next few days frantically looking for the dog, putting up posters, knocking on doors, and speaking to everyone they could. Unfortunately, they did not have any luck. The mother of the family had read a story in a local newspaper about another dog I had found, so she gave me a ring to ask me if I could help find her dog Ralph. I enquired if they felt he had fallen over the cliff, and she assured me that, if he had fallen over the cliff, he would have died. It was a horrendous drop. She was adamant that he had not gone over the cliff. I asked for his photograph and his name, and I told her I would communicate with him.

As soon as I received the photograph, I connected to him. I could see a very high cliff with a waterfall or stream cascading over. As I looked, I saw where the dog had fallen. He was near a beach; however, it was a long way over the rocks, and rescuers would have to go through the sea to get to him. I breathed a sigh of relief, knowing where he was and that he was still alive. As I thought, he had fallen over the cliffs. Goodness knows how he had survived, but he had, and he was understandably very frightened. The dog was lying on a small ledge and showed me how afraid he was of the water when the tide came in. The weather had been reasonable, but was set to change for the worse. I gave Ralph's guardian the location, but unfortunately, she did not believe me. They went to the area and called out to the dog, but could not get any response. They returned home, and a week or so later my husband was reading the *Western Morning News* newspaper, when an article stating that the Royal National Lifeboat Institution (RNLI) had been called out to rescue two young men who had gone cliff climbing and had landed on some rocks and got cut off by the tide in gale-force conditions. When the rescue team got there, they learned that the men had found a stranded dog, and they asked if the dog could go in the boat with them. The dog, at this stage, was really frightened because of the wind and water. The RNLI team said it was too dangerous because of the weather and the way the dog was playing up. It was decided to leave him for the safety of everyone else. My husband said, 'Maureen, I think this is the dog you found.' I rang the guardian and read the article out to her and told her where he was. She got in touch with an animal rescue charity, and they in turn contacted the helicopter service to go out and locate the dog. To our great relief, they found him and tempted him with sandwiches into a sling so that they could fly him back to safety and get the vet to check him over. His guardian was informed, and they came down and picked him up. Sometime later, the guardian, who ran a magazine that was all about horses, decided to invite everyone who had helped to rescue her dog to a celebration buffet. To our delight, she invited the helicopter pilots and requested they bring the video footage. The footage showed that he had fallen a long way down the cliff. The pilot said that Ralph was a very lucky dog. He had not been visible from the ground, and it had taken a great effort to locate him from the air. After we watched the video, the husband came up to me and told me that they had totally given up on Ralph and had even got another dog. He thanked me enthusiastically and told me they now had two dogs, and they were thrilled to have Ralph back.

Dogs Alert Me to Entity in Their Home

A lady contacted me when she became very upset because her two red setters were misbehaving badly. I communicate with them, and they told me that there was a bad entity in the house. They had been trying to tell their guardian, but she was not listening. I told the dogs that she couldn't hear them, and I promised I would come down and sort it out. I spoke to the lady and explained that I needed to visit to cleanse her home and find the issue. She said that it was fine; however, she would be at work. Her husband would be there to let me in for the cleansing, but he was very skeptical. My first thought was, *Here we go again!*

I drove down to their house, and when I arrived, her husband looked at me a bit strangely. I asked him to walk round the house with me and simply ignore what I was doing. He agreed. Just as I was about to investigate quite a nice big walk-in wardrobe in an upstairs bedroom, their telephone rang downstairs. I told him he could go and answer it, which he did. I approached the wardrobe and opened the door. As I did, a boot was thrown at me and it hit me on the head. Great! I had found where the entity was, so with the archangel's help, I put him into the light. This stopped the dogs' bad behaviour immediately, and the guardians were very grateful to have a happy, peaceful house once again.

Requesting Help for a New Friend

I was running a horse show for my charity. I had been rushing around all over the place organising everything. As I walked past the entry tent, I noticed a lady with two sheltie dogs. She was watching the show jumping. I was taken aback when one of the dogs spoke to me: 'Excuse me. Excuse me. Can I talk to you?' I stopped and asked what the problem was. 'I need to have a word with you. We have a problem.' He gave me a brief explanation.

I said, 'Okay. Just give me a minute.' I tapped the lady on the shoulder and said, 'Excuse me. I do animal communication, and your little sheltie has told me that there is a problem. He tells me that the other dog is new, and he is causing an issue.'

She replied, 'Yes, he is new. I've had him for only a couple of weeks.'

I said, 'Well there is a problem with your dog, I don't know what it is, but please, if you send me a photograph along with his name, I will communicate with him and tell you what is wrong.' I gave her my email address.

When I communicated with the dog, I learned that there were several issues. The dog was missing a companion dog who had died. He was grieving not only for this other dog, but also for his natural mum and his siblings. Moving forward, I was able to teach that dog how to communicate with these animals, alive and passed, no matter where they were in the world or in the higher realm. I took the dog through the process, explaining to him that he was in a new home, and it was a very good home. The dog agreed and added that he was being well cared for. He was unsettled only because he was missing the others. I reminded him by saying, 'This is your way of communicating with them now. You will be able to talk with them when you need to.' I then asked, 'Are you happy now?' He told me he was, and I was then able to give his new guardian all the information so she could understand what had been said between the dog and me.

I am often accosted when I am out; sometimes I am busy, but sometimes I'm not. Animals recognise that I am able to do this sort of communication, and very often they are guided to me.

Entity Attachment

Quite frequently, I hold healing sessions at a friend's indoor schooling facility. I schedule half-hour appointments for anyone who wants to bring an animal to see me. It is usually all dogs, and this story is about the last dog that came in on one particular day. I noticed he was high stepping like a Nazi soldier. He had the strangest walking gait, and when I got into his energy, it didn't feel right, so I came back out very swiftly. I informed the guardians that they had challenging entities in their home, and I needed to visit their home and cleanse it. I suggested we make our way there immediately so I could remove the entity for them. The husband's reply was one of gratitude.

The couple lived down near Redruth at the southern tip of Cornwall, and when we arrived, I noticed many awards won by their six lovely collie dogs in competitions.

When I began opening up and tuning in to the dogs, I immediately saw the spirit of a man. I looked at the daughter and said to her, 'You see spirits. Do you see a man when you come out during the night?'

'Yes," she said. 'I am scared of him, he frightens me. I rush out to go to the toilet and then rush straight back in again.'

I said, 'Okay we can move him on.' I set about moving him into the light with the help of the archangels. As I started the cleansing of the home, I suddenly found myself down in a mine looking at sixteen dear lost souls who hadn't crossed over. As I was looking around, the tunnels began to open up in all directions. I found myself going along the tunnels, experiencing an abundance of challenging energy spreading in every direction. I called on the archangels again to help me to cleanse the space and release the trapped souls into the light. We got every soul to queue up, and one by one, I counted them into the light until they were all gone. I then found myself back in the house and continued to cleanse the couple's home. When I finished, I said to the guardians, 'My goodness, you must have had horrendous problems here.' They agreed that the electrics had been flickering and other mechanical things had been going wrong for no reason. Unfortunately, the family members couldn't sleep, and they were having frequent arguments, all signs of a bad entity in the house. I told them that it would stop now.

Then I asked them if they realised they were living very close to the mine workings. The husband looked at me and said, 'Do you remember a report last year on television about a house in this area? The middle of the building suddenly just dropped down into a mine shaft.' I told him I'd seen the report. 'Well,' he said, 'that was the house next door. It was just a few yards away from our home. Do you think there's a shaft under our house?'

I told him, 'No, but there's a shaft under their lane, and it goes under the road.'

The husband was so thankful. He said, 'Maureen, I can't thank you enough. I want to kiss you! We have had such horrendous problems with family issues, arguments, the dog's ill health, not sleeping, and electrical faults. Our son's car keeps breaking down, and he has recently been in an accident in that car.' These incidents were all linked to the bad energy that was trapped in their home. Since the cleansing, the dogs are doing well and the energy in and around the home is calm. It is a much happier place to live in.

Angelic Healing

Arnie

A lovely lady had asked me a few times for help with her dogs. On this occasion, Arnie needed some help with his health. He was scratching; some sort of skin issue was affecting his entire body. I communicated with Arnie, and he told me that he had hookworms, and although they had been treated, something had migrated up under his skin. This was what was making him itch, and the scratching was making him raw and causing bald patches over his body.

I called in the archangels to do some healing on him, inside and out, and they told me to tell his guardian to wash him in warm water to open the pores of his skin, and then to cover him completely in garlic oil and to rub it well in. It needed to stay on the skin for an hour. Then she could shampoo him and wash it all off. That would cure the problem by killing everything off. Keep in mind the fact that this lady had taken this dog to the vet. They had given her all sorts of things that hadn't worked.

She did what the angels had advised, and it cured him. His coat grew back, he stopped itching because the symptoms calmed down. She has been back to me again since with something else that is going on with Arnie. I asked if she had been to the vet with him, and she said, 'No. I came to you first because you seem to be able to find out from Arnie himself what is going on.'

I hope with all this there is another way of helping animals so that they do not have to ingest all the toxins that poison their bodies.

Breeding Dog Grieving and Give Up on Life

A lady came to one of my workshops with her dog, a beautiful collie bitch that hadn't been with her for very long. She said, 'I am a bit worried about her. She has switched off. She doesn't play, she doesn't eat. She shows no interest in life whatsoever. I can't find out what is happening with her, and I am a bit concerned.'

When I communicated with her, we found out what the problem was. As soon as I was in her energy, I found myself crying and crying. I asked her, 'What is the matter?'

She said, 'They steal my babies! I hate humans! They steal my babies, and I don't know where they go. I am having babies all the time, and they keep stealing them. I never see them again.'

I said to her, 'I think you may have been living on a puppy farm where they continually breed dogs just to make money by selling the puppies. Your puppies could be anywhere.' When I asked if she communicated with them, she told me she didn't know how to do that. I told her I would show her how to communicate with her own puppies, her mother, and her siblings. She thanked me, and I apologised for humans who had done this to her. I told her that, for them, it was all about money and not about her. I finished by saying, 'You are now in a home with people who love you dearly. Your new guardian wants to take you for walks and feed you lovely food. Take advantage of this new home.'

The lady told me that, when she stopped on the way home to let the dog go out to go to the toilet, the dog bounced around playfully.

The guardian told me she had got the dog from a breeder who told her the dog was no longer of use. The guardian had saved her from that dreadful situation. Now the dog was in a lovely home ready to begin a new happy future.

Again, this is all about humans not caring about what animals feel and experience. They are at the expense of humans who are arrogant enough to think they know best.

Let Me Go!

One day, a lady who was at the end of her tether rang me about her beautiful red setter, one of two sister she owned. The dog had been ill for two years. The guardian had visited the vet constantly and asked in other places for advice, but no one had an answer. Only once did a vet help the dog get over an upset tummy, but the dog was still very poorly.

When I asked the dog what was happening, she said, 'They are poisoning me!' I asked what she meant, and she said, 'Well, I was ill. I had an upset tummy for several days.' I asked why she had an upset tummy, and she said, 'I drank the water from a stream. There was a beaver or otter or something further up the stream, so the germs had come down, and this made me sick.' I asked why her sister didn't become ill, and she told me, 'My sister did not drink from the stream.'

I told her I wanted to do some healing on her, but the dog didn't want me to do it. She told me she was so ill that she just wanted to die. I told her that her guardian wanted to make her better, but she told me she couldn't cope with the healing. She just wanted to be left alone. 'My body can't cope anymore, and the drugs have done a lot of damage to the inside of my tummy. Please tell my guardian I want her to let me go. I need to go.' I told her that I would pass that message on to her guardian.

So, sadly, I had to tell the guardian the dog's wishes. I told her that the upset tummy had had happened a while back and would have cured itself, but because the vet had tried several cures that caused poor reactions in the dog, eventually the body had enough, and the dog had gone beyond helping. The dog really didn't want to be here anymore. I advised her to please say goodbye to the dog and allow it to go with dignity.

It was not an easy thing to do, but animal communication is not always an easy thing to do. Animal communicators usually speak to animals that are abused, have bad health issues, or are being kept alive by their guardians when they really want to go. This is all very draining. We are sensitive, so it upsets us and takes a lot out of us. We communicators can protect ourselves and get help, but we are human. We feel and experience all the emotions the animals share with us. We are sensitives, and once we have tuned into the animal's energy, we are part of the animal, and we feel what they are feeling. It's not easy to tell a guardian that his or her dog has asked to be allowed to die. Thank goodness we can do this for our animals.

Angelic Healing Halts Aggressive Cancer Growth

I was holding a stage-two animal communication workshop, which is for the more experienced animal communicators who have been able to communicate with animals for quite a while. In this workshop, I basically teach the students how to communicate on a deeper level with animals and how to get deeper into their energy to be able to perform psychic operations as well as extra-deep communication to determine what's going on with the animal physically as well as psychologically.

During the workshop, a distraught lady arrived carrying in her arms a beautiful collie dog called Sorrell. Sorrell had been diagnosed by the vet with inoperable cancer. The guardian had been told that Sorrell had only a very short time to live. She asked if I could help, so I suggested that she bring the dog into the workshop. Ten of my very experienced students were there to assist me.

In the workshop we had been learning about psychic operations. The students were prepared, and we all did a psychic operation on Sorrell. It was very emotional. We all had tears flowing through us, which is not unusual when we are in an animal's energy, because we can feel what they are feeling. These are not our tears; they are the tears of the animal, reflecting the animal's sadness. Even the guardian was able to pick up on the power of the day and the energy. It was different, and she found it very emotional as well.

After the psychic operations on Sorrell were completed, I asked all the students, one by one, what shape they thought the tumour was. They all described a pear or lightbulb shape. I had seen the same shape, so I verified that they had got that correct.

After the psychic operation, the guardian thanked us profusely and tucked Sorrell into the car for the ride back home to Cornwall. That evening, she gave me a ring and said she was so pleased because, on the way home, she stopped to let Sorrell have a little wander. Normally she would have to carry her out onto the grass verge to have a pee; however, this time, when she opened the car door, Sorrell jumped out, over to the grass, and proceeded to urinate. For the first time in a while, there was no blood in the urine. The guardian was more than thrilled that dear old Sorrell appeared to be much better. What wonderful news! We had been able to remove the tumour, and I later learned that Sorrell lived for another two and a half years. We were delighted to have given her this extra time. Fantastic!

The Dog We Couldn't Help

Tango was a street dog from abroad who had been taken into a charity. I am not sure what breed, or mixture of breeds, this dog was, but when it stood on its hind legs, it was taller than a human. And it was vicious. So, I considered Tango a dangerous dog because of his height, build, and of course, his strong jaw.

The guardian who had brought him over to England was having trouble with this dog; she was partly afraid of it. When I went to her home to see if I could help this dog, I had to go up some steps to get to her flat. The dog was up above me on the stairs, and it went for me as I approached him. Fortunately, I was carrying a bag that contained all the items I use in my work, and I used it to protect my face, so I was not injured.

The guardian quickly took the dog in, and I told her to keep him in another room as I didn't need him with me. I did my best to communicate with the dog and do some healing. I showed this dear dog Tango the consequences of his actions. I told him that he would be put down if he continued to behave in such an aggressive way. Sometimes, threatening an animal is the only way to get it to change its behaviour. I also pointed out that, if he were labelled officially as a dangerous dog, the guardian would not be allowed to keep him. If he bite and hurt a human or another animal, he would be put down. I gave him all the reasons why he should stop his bad behaviour, but I knew this dog had something else going on. Something wasn't right with his brain, and I warned his guardian that I didn't think he was going to change and that she probably would have to put him down.

This dear lady continued to try and look after Tango, and she tried to domesticate him, but to no avail. Sadly, she eventually did have to put him down. So animal communication does not always turn everything around.

Animals do have free will, and sadly I could not help this one. We can't help every animal on the planet.

Skeptic to Believer

On another occasion, a lady left a phone message for me about her small dog companion Dolly that she'd recently had to have put down. She asked if I could contact Dolly. The lady explained that she was very skeptical of what I do, but I had been recommended to her. This lady was bedridden. She explained that she'd had a toy breed dog that used to stay on the bed with her and keep her company. Dolly was everything to this lady. She asked if I could communicate with the dog. I said yes and asked her to send me a photograph.

I promptly communicated with Dolly, and when I rang the lady to give her the reading, I gave her the various messages that Dolly had given to me. Dolly had given me a vision of some cabbage in a saucepan, and of course the lady was very skeptical. As I continued giving her all the messages she said, 'That's it! I'm sorry, but I don't believe a word of this. It's all rubbish!' I told her that this was the message that Dolly had given, but she was adamant that she and her husband didn't like cabbage, so it could not be true. She went on to say that her husband did all the cooking, and that the weekend before Dolly was put down, he had cooked a roast lunch, but he had burnt the cabbage. I waited for her to realise what she had just said. Then I told her that Dolly knew she didn't like cabbage and that would prove to her that I was speaking to Dolly. Animals are marvellous. Dolly made the connection for me to show her guardian that I was communicating with her on the other side.

Relief From Pain and Suffering Via Energy Healing

Pippa's guardians were worried about her. They had taken the dog to see the vet. She'd had physio and lots of veterinary treatments to get her right.

There was a dreadful smell coming from her skin, she was not walking very freely, and she wasn't able to get up onto her own big armchair. Her guardians had been lifting her up onto it.

Someone had recommended me to the couple, so the lady asked if I could help. I never make promises, but I said I would certainly do my best her.

I did some healing and communication on Pippa, and she gave me a vision of her jumping for a ball. As she jumped, she twisted her spine. I could see that the nerves were all damaged. I said, 'I will do my best to help you, Pippa.' I did two sessions of healing because the damage was so extensive.

Within a week after the second treatment, I received a phone call from her guardian. She told me that they were thrilled to bits. Pippa was running around. She was free of pain and there was no stiffness. She was now jumping up onto her own chair and was the dog she had been before her injury. It was so wonderful that Pippa was now leading her normal life and out of pain.

Lost Sukie Enjoying Freedom

Another animal that I was asked to help was a Terrier called Sukie. Her guardians had taken Sukie to their usual walking spot up by East Salterton in Devon. They stopped the car, opened the boot, and Sukie jumped out. The guardian turned to get something out of the boot, and when she turned around again, Sukie had gone. She called and shouted and rushed around looking for her, but could not find Sukie. The guardian was convinced that Sukie had been stolen. She believed that someone had picked her up and put her in their car. It is a popular visitor location, and there were a lot of vehicles in the carpark. A week or so had gone by before the guardian contacted me after someone recommended that she get in touch with me. So, after receiving a photograph of Sukie, I communicated with her.

Sukie showed me a riverbank. I could see a line of poplar trees; an old, upturned dinghy boat; and a sluice gate. I asked Sukie if that was where she was. 'Yes!' she said. 'I have been going up and down here.' I asked her to show me where else she was going, and she showed me a stone bridge. Then she showed me some shops, and I could see her eating. When I asked her what she was eating she told me it was something that some people had thrown away. She was hungry. I asked her to show me what it was, and I could see that it was part of a pasty. I told her that I was trying to locate her so that her guardian could find her. When they were reunited, her guardian would feel her properly and keep safe and warm.

Sukie wasn't very interested in this, and I realised that, by now, Sukie had clicked back into being the feral dog that she would have been in the wild. She was enjoying what I call 'a jolly', away from the energy of the guardian without any restrictions. Sukie was not lost. She knew what she was doing, she was avoiding her human!

I asked Sukie if she had heard her guardian calling her, and she told me she had. I asked her where she had been when she was being called, and she said she was down a rabbit hole. She also told me that she was not ready to go home yet. I told her that I would let her guardians know.

When I told the guardian what Sukie had told me, she said that she was not sure about what I'd said. I asked her what she meant. She said that Sukie followed her everywhere, even when she went to the bathroom. I told her that she had to realise that this was a dog who was having a taste of life as it would be without humans. I relayed the message that she would come home to her, but she was not ready yet. She was having a doggy holiday, enjoying life.

This went on for almost three months, and then the weather changed. I next communicated with Sukie during a snowstorm. The wind was blowing, and it was cold. When I got into Sukie's energy, I mentioned that it was cold out there, and she agreed. She was cold and hungry and wanted to go home. I told her that I would put a lead on her in the etheric sense and give the other end to her human guardian. I asked Sukie to please walk back in the direction that felt right to her. I advised that, if she felt she was going in the wrong direction, she was really going wrong. If the direction felt right, then it was right. I told her that her human guardian would meet her and take her home.

Before the guardian had gone all the way up the track, she came across two ladies who had Sukie on a lead. She greeted them and said, 'Thank you!

That's my dog, Sukie. She has been lost for quite a while.' They said that they had been walking up the riverbank and had seen the dog coming in the opposite direction. 'We were intrigued because no one was with it,' said one of the ladies. 'But it seemed to know where it was going and what it was doing.'

When they got further up by a bridge, they noticed the poster for a missing dog. They turned around and came back to catch up with her dog. They put a piece of string around Sukie's neck and walked in the direction it had been going to see where it was heading. 'Now we have met,' said the other lady, 'we at least know she is going home safely.'

Sukie had returned home, and the guardians were extremely grateful.

Although I had been giving them messages, they still had nagging thoughts that she may have been stolen or, worse, was dead. They could not get over the fact that what I had told them was the truth. Soon they were reunited and all back safely in the warm.

Tasha's Communication from Spirit

As soon as Tasha came through, I could feel a very kind, calm, and loving energy. She told me that she had crossed over and that a beautiful angel had come forward to take her to the other side. She was pleased because she was not sure what was going on. But she was soon put at her ease.

Tasha said that she had several of her family members waiting for her when she arrived; in fact, she was amazed there were so many. Some she had not met before, but she was completely relaxed and able to adjust to it all. They made sure she was welcome. Tasha told me they were quite the pack now and had no need for a pack leader as all of them worked as one unit.

Tasha gave me a vision of her guardian holding her head low and crying. She asked me to tell her guardian to walk tall, hold her head high, dry her eyes, then look to the sky. The guardian would be shown a cloud that was shaped like a dog, and this would be Tasha letting her know she would always be with her.

Tasha also said she visited her guardian at night when she was asleep and stayed on the bed with her. She then gave me the sound of snoring, but I was not sure if this was Tasha or her guardian snoring!

Tasha wanted her guardian's tears of sadness to turn to tears of joy. She wanted her guardian to remember all the good times, as they were soul mates and had already had two lives in the past together, and with this life, that made three soul journeys.

Next, she gave me a vision of her digging the sand on a beach and then jumping to catch a ball. She said she could do this sort of thing now because she was fit and well and happy again and just wanted her guardian to understand that she could not have changed anything; it had been Tasha's time to go. Tasha then gave me a vision of three ladies and a gentleman who were family members in spirit that were with her. They said they were also watching over Tasha's guardian and trying to help, but she was grieving and blocking any help they could give to her. They asked her to please try to open up so that Tasha and her family members could assist her with her journey here on earth.

Lastly, Tasha said that the colour purple was significant for her and her guardian. She asked me to ask the guardian to keep this colour near to her as much as possible because the energy of purple would help the guardian make a better connection to her.

Guidance For Luna

As I tuned into Luna's energy, I felt on full alert ready to react to anything. She was in full protective mode. Luna was grieving for her natural mum and siblings, so I set about showing her how she could communicate with them, whether they were alive or deceased. Luna thanked me for this. I asked Luna why she was always on full alert, and she gave me a vision of her past life as a wolf in a pack. Her position in the pack was next to the Alpha, and she was responsible to ensure that the pack was protected by alerting them of any threats by any other wolf packs entering their territory. Unfortunately, Luna had brought this understanding forward into her present life and was not experiencing what it is like to be in a domestic pack, meaning a pack that included humans. When Luna went out on walks, she would react very quickly to any other dogs that came within her view. She was ready to defend her human pack who were her alphas in this life. This reaction was an automatic response and instinctive to her. She would find it difficult not to respond to her Instincts because it meant survival in her past life.

I explained to Luna what happens in a domestic situation like the one she was currently in: going to the toilet only in the garden and on walks rather than in the home, making sure not to damage any furniture in the home, and refraining from going into protection mode when she saw other dogs from the car, house, or out on walks.

I then sent her a vision that showed her how she could greet other dogs calmly, with all four paws on the ground, with jaw shut, and without barking or biting. I said she should greet them relaxed with her tail wagging. She could sniff them, and they would sniff her with their tails wagging. At that point, she would have made a friend. This would entice other dogs to come and play, which would be much better than threatening them. This behaviour would make life more enjoyable for her and her human family, who were currently stressed out every time any dog approached on a walk, in the car, or in the house.

I then spoke to Luna about children who approached her. I told her that she was a very beautiful dog, and lots of children would want to say hello and smooth her. I then advised her that, when children approached her, she should keep all her four paws on the ground, and she should wag her tail. I asked her not to jump up at them as that could frighten the children, especially if they were pushed to the ground. I asked her to please allow them to smooth her and make friends with her. This would be so much more enjoyable than being in protective mode continually.

I asked her to remember that her guardians were the alphas in her current domestic pack, and they would give her food and care for her, so she did not need to be so protective when it was not needed. She could be protective only when threatened by someone who was not giving off a good energy or aura.

When I was communicating with Luna, I could feel a strange energy around her shoulders, neck, and head. It was caused by her pulling on the lead. I then showed her how she could walk on a lead and never have to pull, so she wouldn't hurt her guardian, and she wouldn't hurt her neck

I asked Archangel Michael to cut the cords from Luna's past life and this life that she no longer needed. Once the cord cutting had finished, I felt a lot of release sensations. Archangel Michael said that she had held onto lots of chords that were not required. I downloaded a full body healing on her and took all the trauma energy out of her body. Luna is now a much more domesticated dog, and she understands she is not living in her past life. She is also a lot happier and more content.

Cat Communication Stories

I am Not Lost

Yogi the cat and his guardians lived in in a flat Plymouth. The guardians needed help because Yogi had not been home for several days. They were worried that he was lost. They asked if I would communicate with him and make sure he was still alive and okay. I got into Yogi's energy and said, 'I believe you're lost.'

'No,' he said, 'I am not lost. I know where I am.'

I said, 'Sorry. I was told you were lost. You haven't been home.'

'No. I am out doing what I want to do.'

I asked him if he was far from home. He said that he wasn't lost and that he knew his way home. I told him that I didn't wish to upset him, but his guardians were worried about him. He told me that he was fine and that he would go home when he was ready. It was wonderful to be able to tell his guardians that he was not lost. Sure enough, about a week later, Yogi turned up meowing and asking for the window to be opened. The guardian immediately phoned me to let me know that Yogi had returned home, and she was thrilled to bits. She could not believe it. One lost cat that wasn't lost.

I am in the Wrong Designated Home

My friend rang me to say that a stray had turned up at her house. She had cats of her own, but this stray was insisting on coming into her house. She said that she was worried because it belonged to someone else, and she didn't want those people to worry. I communicated with this dear cat, my friend called him Tommy, and he told me that this was where he belonged, with this guardian. I asked him if he had been at another home. 'Yes! And it was the wrong home,' he said. 'This is where I am meant to be. This is where my soul journey is.' I told him that I would let my friend know.

When I told her, she said that she couldn't keep someone else's cat, so I suggested that she try to find the cat's guardian and explain. I knew full well that not everyone believes in what I do and what I have to say.

So, she did find the guardian and discovered that Tommy had walked quite a long way, crossing over an extremely busy road, a road that was quite dangerous for an animal to cross. The lady came and took Tommy back home, but a few days later, he turned up at my friend's house again. So, she rang the original guardian, who once again picked up Tommy and took him back home. But within a week, Tommy was back at my friends again. 'So!' I said to her, 'I told you he says that he is meant to be with you, not with them.'

I suggested she had better have a word with the original owners as he was going to continue to run away, and he might be killed crossing the very busy road. So, they had a word, and the original lady decided that my friend should keep Tommy. It was safer for him to stay with his new owners even though she loved him dearly and would miss him. So, Tommy was allowed to stay with my friend and live out his soul's journey.

Seeing is Believing

A lady from Scotland contacted me. She had a Persian cat called Lulu who was twenty years old, a wonderful age, but she had an ulcer in one of her eyes. The eye was all cloudy. The vet had given her antibiotics and eye drops, but none of it was working, and the eye was not healing. She asked if I could help, and I told her that I couldn't make promises, but I would do my very best. She promised to send me a photograph.

I used my wand and concentrated my healing on Lulu. This was long distance healing from Devon to Scotland! The guardian of the cat rang me about a week later and said she could not believe it, the eye had recovered, not fully, but was 80 per cent better, and it was not causing all the problems that it had been. The lady was thrilled to bits with the healing that I had done. Lulu's eye eventually fully recovered, so that was fantastic.

Barney: Goes on A Journey

Barney lived in Wales. He was a house cat who didn't go out; he stayed indoors. His guardian called me. She frantic because he had been missing for three nights. She had searched everywhere, been around to all the neighbours, put posters out. She was worried because Barney had no life skills for surviving outdoors.

I communicated with Barney, and I asked him what route he had taken when he left the house. He told me that he had gone out the front door and turned left. I asked him to show me where he was. It looked as if he was hiding under some sort of shed. I asked him if he was hungry, but he said he wasn't as there was a lady giving him food. I asked him to show me the lady. I could see this lady in a blue top and a blue cardigan. As I got the vision, the angels said to me, 'She's been to the doctor, and she hasn't long come back.'

I thanked the angels and then phoned Barney's guardian. I told her that she needed to go out of her front door and turn left and look for somewhere close by. One of her neighbours would be wearing blue and had just come home from the doctor. She went to see her next-door neighbour and showed her a photo of Barney, and then asked if she had seen him. Her neighbour said that she had been feeding him for a few days. The neighbour also told her that she was lucky to have caught her in, she had just returned from the doctors. When the guardian went into her neighbour's back garden, she found Barney under a wooden building. Barney has now gone back to being a house cat once again and is safe at home and in the arms of his caring guardian.

Stanley: The Explorer

Another cat was lost. Bless them, cats tend to do this. They are much more independent than dogs. This cat was called Stanley, and his guardian said he had been missing for two weeks. I asked her to send a photograph to me, and when it arrived, I communicated with Stanley who showed me a graveyard that wasn't far from where this lady lived. I asked him what he was doing down there. Stanley told me that he was fine, and that he was catching and eating mice and other things. He showed me a building that looked as if it was partly derelict, but he was in an area of Plymouth called Central Park, the location of the Plymouth Argyle football ground. There used to be a zoo there, but it is abandoned. I assumed that this was the building I was seeing.

I relayed this information to Stanley's guardian who told me that she had moved from her flat and bought her own house, which meant she had to travel a distance every day to the flat where she used to live because she felt that was where Stanley would go. After doing this for about a week, a police car stopped her. The gentleman who now lived in her old flat thought she was up to something suspicious, so he had rung the police and reported her and her vehicle. She explained to the policeman that she was not stalking the man. Her cat had gone missing, and she had since moved from that flat to her new home. She explained she had used an animal communicator and that I had told her that the cat was in this area. She was just driving back every day to see if she could find Stanley. The policeman said that he covered that area, and he would go up around the training area for Plymouth Argyle and mention it to the people there and see if they had seen Stanley.

Sure enough, one of the trainers told the policeman that he had seen the cat on and off hanging around the old zoo buildings. The policeman told Stanley's guardian that her cat was alive, and he was in the area where I had told her he was. The guardian took a cage and some food and sat on the bank where she had been told he'd been seen. When Stanley came through the gap in the hedge, he saw her. He hissed at her because he had been missing for seven months and twelve days. He had turned feral. His guardian patiently sat and talked to him, and eventually he came to the food bowl, she then immediately scuffed him, put him into the cage, and took him home. He was finally reunited with his companion who had been missing him.

Gordon: The Spiritual Teacher

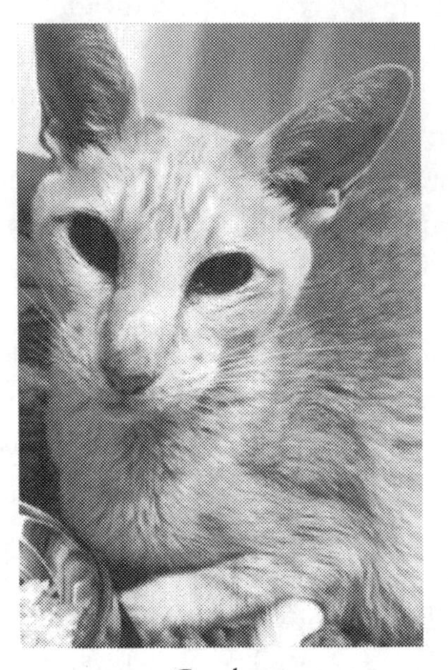

Gordon

A Burmese-Siamese cat called Gordon was such a character, but he was causing problems because he was urinating everywhere. If anyone visited with a handbag he would urinate on it. If anyone put anything down, he would urinate on it.

His guardian asked me to communicate with him to find out why. When I finally got into his energy, I asked him what was going on, he said, 'Oh, thank goodness! At last, someone I can talk to who will listen to me. I have been trying to get her attention.'

I replied, 'What, by urinating everywhere?'

'Yes!" he said. 'It's the only way I can get her attention. She doesn't listen to me. I have been trying to warn her.' I told him that his guardian had asked me to talk to him. What did he want her to know? 'Well,' he said, 'It's her mum in spirit. She is upset, and quite honestly so am I.' I asked him why. 'Well, she is working herself to death. She is working at least two jobs; she comes home and then dashes out again.' He also said that she was away for periods of time and no one saw her 'She is running herself into the ground, and quite honestly, her health is suffering because of it. If she doesn't stop, she will be seriously ill.' He also asked me to tell his guardian that her mum has asked that she stop wasting her money on flowers and visiting the cemetery because her mum is not there. His final message was to tell his guardian that the thing she is looking for is under the dresser.

I contacted the guardian and told her all of this. She laughed, as she was a veterinary nurse working all hours. She was also helping clients with their animals at their houses, and she was house sitting for their animals. So, she was doing two jobs and she was staying on looking after animals while people were on holiday or in hospital. I told her that she needed to slow down, to work fewer hours and to make sure that she rested up. As soon as she did all this, Stanley stopped urinating everywhere, and she was thrilled to bits, so she started to put things back out and around the way she had them before Stanley started 'misbehaving'.

A few weeks later, she phoned me to tell me that he had started again. I asked if she had been working long hours again and she said she had. I told her to slow down and relax, and he would stop. 'It's Gordon's way of reminding you to take care of yourself,' I told her. I just love doing animal communications as they teach us so much about ourselves and about what's going on around us

After I worked with Gordon and his guardian, I received a visit from Archangel Gabriel who appears every so often when I need to have information. He said the archangels wanted me to perform healing on humans as well as communicating with animals. Sadly, my experience working with humans up to that point in time had not been good. Humans were the ones who were abusing animals, especially the ponies I used to rescue. I have seen the dreadful side of humans, all the negative. Owners as well as dealers can be dreadful people who do awful things to animals. So, my usual belief was, give me animals any day. I prefer them to humans. So, when Archangel Gabriel asked me to do healing on humans, my automatic response was no, no, and no! Archangel Gabriel said yes and then disappeared.

I decided that I would just carry on with the animals. I should have known better; the angels are fantastic, and they work wonders in many ways. Well, they have certainly done that with me, because the next four animals that came to me next had problems with their humans. I would not be able to resolve the animal's issues until I had worked on their humans. Only then would the animals behave themselves.

Gordon was one of these animals. After I worked with him, I did healing on his guardian to help her calm down, and Gordon stopped urinating. I told her where that item was that had been lost, and sure enough it was under the dresser where Gordon had said. Fantastic. Just love it!

I now do healing on humans as well as animals and have been doing so for several years. To be honest, I must say that it is equally as rewarding as healing animals. The archangels have taught me a lesson about judging others and making decisions when I have not truly manifested the intention of seeing both sides. Just like animals, humans are all different, so I have been taught a lesson: I must see beyond the issue and see what lies within, and I must treat every human and every animal as an individual.

So, I thank Archangel Gabriel, all the archangels who are helping me, all my guides, and our dear Lord God as well.

Tayo's Experience of The Dark Side to Humans

I was contacted by a lady called Joanne who was very upset. She had taken her cat Tayo to the vet the day before because he was having trouble breathing. She had let him out earlier that day and he was fine, but when he returned home, he was in a very bad way.

The vet examined him and could not find any reason for his breathing problems, but they kept him overnight for observation and treatment. Joanne was upset and very concerned for her Tayo. She asked me if I could communicate with him and perform healing on him urgently. Unfortunately, I was not feeling very well, and communication was not possible, but I did heal Tayo immediately.

Next morning, I set about communicating with Tayo. He was very unbalanced and all over the place. He also was very frightened and in a state of trauma. When I entered his energy, I had trouble breathing, and I could feel a lot of pain all over my body, particularly in my chest, lungs, stomach, and arms (which would be Tayo's front legs). All these feelings I experienced were what Tayo was feeling.

Tayo tried to show me something, but at first, I was not able to receive because his energy kept breaking the link and then coming back. This happened twice while I was in his energy, and the angels told me he kept leaving his body, and they were returning him. Tayo was finally able to show me a man's boot. It was a pale camel colour and very large. The boot kicked Tayo hard against the wall numerous times. He had been beaten nearly to death.

I asked Tayo to fight for his life and told him that Joanna was extremely upset at what had happened to him. She just wanted him to fight to stay alive and not let go. I said I would help him and do healing with the archangels, but he needed to fight to live.

I apologised for what the dreadful man had done to him and told him that the archangels would sort that man out for his despicable actions on a defenceless animal.

After establishing that Tayo did not communicate with his natural mother and siblings, I showed him how he could talk to her about what had happened to him so that she can give him a mother's love as well. I then ended the connection with a full and detailed healing on Tayo's body, paying particular attention to the areas that he was having most trouble with.

I explained to Joanne what I had learned, and I told her that Tayo had a fifty-fifty chance of survival. She was in tears, and she told me that, at the same time I was communicating with Tayo, she had asked the vet to X-ray his chest. Unbeknown to me, the vet told Gemma that Tayo had taken a beating. His lungs were extremely bruised, as were some of his other organs, and he had a fifty-fifty chance of surviving.

I continued to do healing daily on Tayo, and early in 2020 Tayo, came home from the vet, but his front paw was paralysed. I carried on performing healing on Tayo to see if we could get the paw working correctly; however, sadly, Tayo finally went over the rainbow bridge.

Izzy Sensitive to EMF

When I tuned into Izzy's energy, I felt sick, and my body was tingling and itchy. She gave me the sense I was smelling something. It smelled like electricity. I then quickly realised what Izzy was giving me, it was indications of an electromagnetic field (EMF) emanating from something electrical.

Izzy said she could feel the EMF, and was affecting her negatively. She had been trying to get her guardian's attention so she could let her know that this was affecting everyone's health in the home, not just Izzy's.

EMFs emanates from electrical apparatus—computers, tablets, microwaves, mobile phones, gaming consoles, fairy lights, connectors, fish tank lights, and smart meters to name a few. Pylons, electrical poles, and electrical boxes that can also cause EMFs to enter your home

You can block EMFs by placing shungite crystals near all your electrical equipment. You can also carry shungite with you to block EMFs on your body, or you can place one under your pillow at night. If there are pylons or electricity poles or boxes near your home, place shungite crystals in the windows facing the pylons to block the EMFs coming into your home.

Periodically cleanse the shungite crystals by smudging with burning sage or by holding them under a cold-water tap. Let the water run down the drain so no one can drink it.

I told Izzy's guardian that Izzy was showing aggression in an attempt to get their attention and warn them about the EMFs. She had been getting frustrated as she felt her guardians were not listening to her warning. Izzy was a kind, gentle soul, and she was just trying to protect her guardian and her family.

Izzy expressed that she was also missing her natural mum and siblings; sadly, she was grieving for them. I explained to her how she could communicate with them all, whether they were alive or deceased. Although she was missing her natural mother, Izzy was very happy and felt a very strong connection to her human guardians. She asked me to thank each one of them for their love and constant care.

It is my belief that Izzy is an old soul that has been on this planet in multiple past lives. She has come back in this life to help, guide, and protect her guardians and to ensure their safety.

Chapter 8

CONCLUSION

Writing this book has allowed me to reconnect with a lot of the animals that I have had the pleasure of talking to and helping with what has been happening in their lives.

Each one has been a journey, and I have been able to learn from all the communications I have done throughout my life on this wonderful animal communication and healing journey.

It has, at times, been very emotional and very humbling to be allowed into the energy and lives of these animals. They have told me about their fears, anguish, pain, and abuse. Sometimes they have even left scars on my heart. But, likewise, I have felt the unconditional love and the caring and healing nature of these dear animals as well.

Their forgiving nature is truly amazing. Many who have been abused badly are still willing and able to give unconditional love to new guardians.

Some animals are amazing healers and have shown me the care and healing they have done on their guardians. This is truly the love and connection that is meant for all human guardians and their wonderful animals. Many humans and their animals have been soul mates in past lives; the connection is so strong that losing one another is like losing part of their hearts and bodies.

I want to thank you all for taking the time to read my book. I hope you have found it informative and helpful as you relate it to what you may be experiencing and feeling. After all, we are all born with our brains free from constraints, and we are all animal communicators and healers in varying degrees.

And finally, I want to thank all the archangels, angels, our dear Lord God, and higher beings in the higher realm along with all my guides and my unicorn guide, Sirius. All have helped and supported me throughout my entire life and ensured that I wrote this book for many to read and experience.

I would also like it to be noted that the references to vets in my book are from my clients and not to reflect my personal view. I have, over the years, developed great respect for the many vets I have had to call on to help animals in distress, as well as my personal pets and the moorland ponies, I cared for through the South West Equine Protection organisation.

My love and angel light to you all.

Printed in the United States
by Baker & Taylor Publisher Services